MW00398023

Afghan hearts & minds

Shafie Ayar

CROWN OAK PRESS

Copyright © 2010 by Shafie Ayar

Afghan hearts & minds
by Shafie Ayar

Printed in the United States of America

ISBN 9781612150222

All rights reserved solely by the author. The author guarantees all contents are original and do not infringe upon the legal rights of any other person or work. No part of this book may be reproduced in any form without the permission of the author. The views expressed in this book are not necessarily those of the publisher.

In the year 2001, shortly after 9-11, the American Congress approved twenty billion dollars for the Afghan War. Afghanistan was occupied, the Taliban were toppled, Osama and his friends were dispersed. Now nine years later, in the middle of a financial crisis at home, with millions of us are losing our houses, we have spent 430 billion dollars more. The only thing we know for certain now, is that we are in deep trouble.

Was that twenty billion dollars just a miscalculation, or is the 430 billion dollars what we are paying for our mistakes?

Well, come with me, as I take you for an interesting short trip to Afghanistan. I promise you that at the end of the trip you will know what is truly going on.

Let me see, where should we start? I think I will take you to my home to introduce you to my family, before we go out.

Knock, knock...

My brother Khalil was two years older than me. My sister Parween, the eldest of all of us was two years older than Khalil. Rona, my younger sister was two years younger than me. Rahmath, my younger brother, was two years younger than her. Ehsan, my other younger brother; two years younger than Rahmath. My youngest sister Farah, and finally my youngest brother Frough. As if it was designed in a lab, one girl and then two boys, again one girl and two boys, two years between us all.

If I were to try and encapsulate the woman who brought these brothers and sisters into the world in one way, it would be that she is a woman full of energy—like a bee. But really, my mother's energy is far more than that of a mere bee. Bees rest in at night, but not her. She was always the last one to sleep, and in the morning she was the first one to rise—and we did not sleep in! She made sure of that. And before she had awoken me and my two older siblings, she had already taken care of many chores.

As soon as we were awake, she would help us with our home-work. For a woman with but a tenth grade education, she was surpris-ingly able to help us in mastering every field: math, Dari (our native language), the Quran, and all our other subjects. In an hour she was waking my other siblings and helping them the same way. She then helped all of us to fold our mattresses and blankets, putting them in the little *pas khana* we used for storage. We were like all Afghans, who did not have enough room to let our sleeping places lie flat throughout the day. Between the entire family we only had two little rooms. During the daytime these were our family and living rooms. At night, they were transformed into crowded bed rooms.

We did not work at a desk, but on our beds. As we did so, in between answering our questions, my mother quickly made the breakfast—a simple cup of tea and piece of bread. We would usually use our sugar allowance by stirring it into the morning tea: about one tablespoon for each of us per day was the quota. My older brother and I would often try to sneak another half spoonful, which would make our breakfast truly an affair. That sugar… I think mother was ordering it from heaven! For many years I have used the sugar here in America, and it does not taste like ours did then. A friend once asked me what spice gave the best taste to food. "Hunger," I said, "a spice I have known all my life."

Food was scarce, really scarce. We always had at least one bite too little, and our stomachs always ached throughout the day. That was just a part of life, and not uncommon among our friends. After breakfast the eldest of us began dressing up for school as my mother dressed the younger ones. School started at about eight and was done by around noon. Our schools were all separated and up to six miles from each other. Although the buses were private, they didn't charge the younger kids, well, until you turned fourteen or fifteen. At that age my school was about five miles away and there was many a morning when Mom told me she had no money that day. Without hesitation, I just walked. So did my older brother. The school the others went to was about a mile and half away, so they walked too. Mom always had money for my older sister though.

So we left one by one in the morning, depending on how long it would take us to get to school, followed in a hurry by my mother. Unlike most women in Afghanistan, she worked outside of the home in addition to her role in the home. I still remember what a rush she was always in when walking to the bus station, about a mile and half from home, in order to get to work on time at the girl's high school where she worked as a clerk. I picture her as always racing herself, trying to do things that little bit faster. Or I picture her running towards Noah's Ark as it was about to board for forty days at sea, leaving her to drown.

Just as we left at different times, we arrived home at different times, but we always arrived the same way: hungry, really hungry. Mom knew that. She always rushed home in the same way she did in leaving for the morning. Bursting into the house, she immediately went to light the fire in the backyard. She always struggled a little with that, and it was an added stress that she had to be careful not to put more wood on than necessary. Wood, like sugar, was expensive. Sometimes we helped her, but many times we acted tired and complained about how long our days had been. Then, every day, she would need a bit of scrap paper to get the fire going, so we would look in our notebooks to see what work had already been completed and wasn't really needed anymore. Out those pages would go, into our mother's hands, and into the fire. The worst days were those when the wood was not yet dry enough, and her eyes would get very red and watery from smoke.

She was an excellent chef – really she was. All the relatives were always loudly admiring her meals. I still don't know how a lot of them knew how good she was able to cook, because Mom was uneasy about sharing our food with anyone except her younger sister, our favorite aunt, and sometimes her younger brother, our cheap uncle. My Mom was very stern about never having guests, and in those days I was very unhappy about this. Now, of course, I know it was only because she did not have one extra bite for anybody else.

Most of the time our lunch was composed of a rice dish cooked with a little bit of green lentils called *shola*. *Shola* was one of my favorites, especially when we had the money to buy some yogurt. Mom would mix the yogurt into some crushed garlic and salt, so we could add a little to our bites as we went. That little bit of yogurt and garlic added so much to the food. Some days she would cook *chalo* instead: a white rice dish but you would need to make a stew to go with it. A couple of times a week she would even make a lamb stew: now that was really something. Sometimes lunch was just a *dal*: a stew made from a mixture of lentils. With no refrigerator, of course, meals were cooked one at a time. Sometimes how good mother cooked just made it harder on us, as not only did we need more for our stomachs, but we wanted more as our tongues just watered over the taste. Many reading this might think that we were poor, but by no means was this the case. By the standards of Afghanistan, we were rich. We were among the top twenty percent in our country in terms of wealth.

In the summertime there were more options, even salad. We had these sweet vine ripened tomatoes, which mother would mix up with chopped onion and a dash of salt. We loved cilantro especially, and when summer came we had plenty of that. It was our summer sugar: the smell of it and the taste were amazing. The days we had salad with our stew were such highlights growing up. Boy did we ever feel like we were kings. I can tell you that I have never eaten anything better than those meals. Nothing can taste as good to me as that food in Kabul – that most important spice is ever missing now.

After lunch my mother cleaned, went out for some shopping, did some sewing, and baked the bread. All this before we came to her with our homework again; or rather, before she was making sure we were actually doing it. My brother and I would then try to sneak outside and see our friends. Mom never liked that, especially when we were playing with the street kids, but it was free and we were just kids — we needed to go out and play. Most of the time in Afghanistan, you are born and raised in the same home your whole life, so neighbors are just like your family. We would banter with one another, always teasing, and if we could manage to find a ball in the middle of that dusty narrow street we would play soccer. When we got a hold of that ball we would always create such a hassle for the people trying to pass by. Often we would play marbles too. Marbles were even more popular because we could all afford to buy a few little glass beads to start with.

As the game begun, we'd take aim at each other's marbles and see if we could hit them. There were no "steelies". We had to have good aim to win the game. Suddenly though we would hear our mother shout, "*Khalil, Shafie, Bachay Sag beayn Khana!*" Out came our mother, invariably upset that we had left the house. If you heard that, you knew she was upset. In Afghanistan, the worst curse is always to call somebody a donkey or a dog, (or a dog's son or donkey's son): that was the worst possible thing you could say, and that is what was flying out of her mouth as she saw us fraternizing away.

Soon enough it was dinnertime, and Mom was cooking again. The summer brought her some reprieve, on those few nights our meal did not have to be baked or boiled. On those nights we had bread and *gandana*. *Gandana* is something like green onion leaves, but a little milder. The leaves are about a foot long and half an inch wide. We would fold each leaf into one-inch sections and eat them with a bite of bread and a little salt. Other times we would eat another stew, of potatoes or spinach, of turbot or a *shorba* (a meat soup). Then again there was homework, and then there was sleep. But as we laid out our beds, Mom was still moving, even as our eyes started to close. Sometimes I think she never slept at all, that she only told us she did so that we didn't feel bad that we weren't helping out. We just weren't able to keep going all the time like she was.

Although... we all knew Mom loved us to death, but she barely ever had anything nice to say to us. She did not kiss, or hug us. She did not have time for that, except if one of us had taken ill. If one of us got sick, you could see her combing our hair with her fingers, massaging our foreheads, our necks, our backs. Then, finally, she would hold you tight, hug you and kiss you, sprinkle you with beautiful words. Suddenly she transformed, taking on yet another face – that of motherly nurse.

In great contrast to this, mother was always so healthy. When I think back, there is not one picture of her in my memory of her being sick. I don't remember even one time or even one day that she laid down and said, "I cannot move today." The only time she took a day or two off was when she was giving birth. I was too young to remember most of the births of my brothers and sisters very well, but I can clearly recall the birth of Farah – the seventh child. We were in our winter house Jalalabad as each of us was preparing to go to sleep for the night.

But at about eight o'clock, she told one of my sisters that she felt the child coming. She told my oldest sister Parween, who was about fourteen at the time, to go and ask our *khala* (aunt) Zyagul, mother's dear friend, to come to the house. Parween went out after her and my Mom went in the other room to prep her bed. Our *khala* came over, and around ten o'clock we heard some screams. That was Mom, and that was it.

The following morning mother was up to make breakfast.

The Afghani work and school week is six days, instead of the five in America. Friday was our day off, but for my mother Fridays were the busiest day of the week. Every other Friday is wash day. She would boil a couple buckets of water and mix them gradually with cold water for her use as she went along. There was a big clay pan called *taghara*, which is used to wash the clothes in. She would add soap and press the clothes together until she felt they were clean. It was too expensive to boil a new batch of water each time, and soap wasn't cheap either, so the same water would be used several times over. Everything was washed twice. My older sister would rinse off the soap with cold water and my younger sister would wring the rinse water out of them, before the clothes were hung on a line to dry. It was the boys' job to haul the water from the well for use by the women. Every time the task took about five hours.

As soon as she was done with the clothes, without any break she would rush to light the fire for lunch. My mother was always an excellent cook, but on Fridays she was exceptional. In Afghanistan we did not have an appetizer, and entrée, and then dessert, or rather, we could not afford such things, and never imagined one could – multiple courses. There was simply the main course, and when the food was done we just sat and enjoyed a cup of tea, or two, or three, or more. You could really say that was our dessert. Our tea was served with sugar, but only the first cup, and only a little sugar, but if we could afford it that day we also loved dried fruits, especially raisins and mulberries (with a dose of walnuts if we were really lucky). *Gur*, a solid piece of candy made from the sugar cane juice, was popular with adults and kids alike. But it was very expensive for us, and came in quite limited amounts. Mom always did her best to treat us on Fridays.

We all ate together, though not at your traditional "dining room table". We did not have a table, in fact, nobody in Afghanistan had a table. Instead, we would lay a piece of cloth on the ground and put the main dish in the center of it, the stew and the salad next to that, and everybody took some, diving into the same pot with our hands. There were no utensils; we simply ate with our hands, with a little bread to help make the meal more filling. We always waited for everybody to be there, and for our mother to give us the green light

"*Besm-e- Allah*," (in the name of God) she would say, and the race began. We would always leave a little extra for the younger ones though. My Mom was always the slowest to eat. She made sure we had enough first. If she felt like we did not have enough, then she filled her stomach with bread instead. It was something that none of us really noticed at the time, but when we realized it later in life it made us look back and marvel at her.

At a certain age mother took each of us aside to teach us how to eat with respect to others. She took me, for example, to the other room after a one meal and explained to me the importance of only eating my share. She told me to look at the food, see how many people there were, and estimate how many bites of food there were to go around, and divide in my head the amount of bites were for me. That, as a matter of fact, was my first math lesson. To this date when we are at dinner or lunch I always make sure not to take more than my share. Not only of the food, with anything that I have to share with others, I've made sure not to have more than my share.

Wash day happened every other Friday, with showering day happening the next Friday. We did not take showers in our own homes, but in a public bath. The *hamam*, as we called it, was a thousand square foot building filled with really hot steam. A huge reserve of cold water and a large 500 gallon vat of hot water were there for the taking. You mixed the hot and cold water together in a bucket to obtain the optimal temperature, and then poured it over your head. We washed ourselves with a rough garment and before your eyes all the dirt and oil would be rubbed away. One's hands and feet were washed with a small piece of igneous or volcanic rock. One's hair was washed with a bit of mineral clay that turned soft in the water. Mother was the one who washed us for the first parts of our lives, as she never felt we would do a good enough job and she did not want her money to go to waste. This process also took about four to five hours.

There were two different *hamam*, one for women and one for men. We went with Mom to the women's *hamam* though. My older brother and I just loved that. The women were naked and we certainly took mental snapshots and brought back stories for the neighbourhood boys. They also had their stories as well, because they were going into the same places. People thought that we were just these little innocent boys, but I have to confess, we were little devils all the way. For boys to be able to go to the women *hamam* there were age restrictions, usually four or five years old was the maximum, but we were still going there when my older brother was seven. Usually our mother also took some bread with her to the *hamam*. She knew that after being there in the *hamam* for three hours or so that we would be hungry. Then, after we were done, she would give us each a small piece. The bread was so good, as we were so ready for it, and it moistened in the steam.

Then one morning something disastrous happened to my older brother as we walked into the *hamam*. As we just entered, this lady came to my mother and told her that my older brother was too old for the women's *hamam*. "You should not bring a boy as old as him to the *hamam*. He is too old to be seeing us without our clothes." While my Mom was busy reasoning with the lady in a very apologetic way, to convince her not to make a big deal out of it, my brother and I both knew that the lady was right. Especially about Khalil, who was two years older than me. Khalil was so nervous about being taken away from this wonderland that he began to act as if he was "special", and completely naïve.

The argument got a little louder and some more women came over to take the side of other woman. Finally Mom gave up. Khalil was about to cry, Mom too. For different reasons of course... my mother because she was afraid her son would not be clean, her son because, well... "Bachem Khalil, take your stuff and go to the *hamam mardana* (men's showers)". Khalil and I, we were always buddies but, at the same time, rivals. I had mixed feelings. I was sad to see him go but at the same time laughing at him, as all his tricks did not work and he was no longer welcome where I was.

I was so happy that there was now something that he needed my help with: he needed to look at this *hamam* through my eyes. "Of course I will share the gasps with you my brother, just go," I chuckled to myself. He had no choice, so he picked up his little things... but then the little bastard put it all on the table. He immediately started begging my mother not to make him go alone, and suddenly my mother turns to me and says, "Shafie Bachem, he is right, take your stuff and accompany your brother." For a moment I was fainting. Everything went dark. He dragged me right down with him, and now neither of us were to be allowed into the Promised Land.

You might be wondering where our father was in of this: was there even a Dad? Yes, there was a Dad. Dad was in the army. Most of the time, especially when we were young, he was working somewhere far away from home. Every month he would come for a couple of days, basically to spawn and then return to the military. He had to though. When you were in the Army, you had no choice in the matter. Most of his time was spent in Jalalabad. Jalalabad was only three hours away by bus, but by Afghani standards this was a world away. We could not afford the trip, and he only had one day a week off like the rest of us. Unlike Mom, Dad, even when he was around, liked to take it easy. He did some of our major shopping, but that was all.

He loved his tea. And I am sure he loved us. But when he was around we were rarely very happy. We loved our Dad, it was not that we did not love him, but he always gave us a hard time. My older brother and I liked to go outside and play with the neighborhood boys. We were very close with them. We played tag, marbles, or sometimes soccer. But my Dad did not want us to go out even for a minute. We always snuck out anyway, but whenever we were caught he would spank us. He always fought with Mom too. We loved her dearly and it was really hard to see it. Sometimes Mom took it easy, but often fought right back. In Afghanistan women were very sub-missive to their husbands, but Mom was a fighter. It was never a physical fight, but the verbal sparring seemingly had no end. Then he would go away for another month.

Jalalabad, where Dad worked, was really hot in the summer, but also really warm in the winter, when Kabul is very cold. We spent most of those winters ourselves in Jalalabad. It was tough to live with Dad, but Jalalabad was like heaven. We were off school during the winters, so there was plenty of free time – for Mom too, as her job was at a girl's high school. Although Mom still made us read and write to be prepared for the following year, we had lots of free time.

From early morning to late in the day we were out playing. Except for kites, we had no other toys, but we still had the time of our lives.

Our lives could not get any better. We played with our neighbours: running, soccer, flying our kites, and when we fought the kites of others to try to cut their strings, we would run for miles after the kites to bring them back. That was a part of childhood, in that corner of the world, every person cherished. Hundreds of kids would go running to get that runaway kite. Sometimes in the competition to grab it and the struggle over it on the ground we would tear the kite into little pieces, but mostly we respected the rights of whoever caught it the first, who kept it as their victory trophy.

This was how it went at home though: at the end of the day before Dad gets home, my brother and I both rush back. Dad hated to see us outside, so we would pretend like we were inside all day. Once in a while we would become so enraptured playing with our friends though that we totally forgot about Dad. The good thing was that Dad never embarrassed us in front of our friends. If he came to see us outside he never shouted at us. He quietly slipped home and just waited there. When it got dark and it was time to go home, we would finally realize that we had forgotten about him, and our hearts would drop.

At that moment we wished we were dead; we were that afraid of our Dad. It was not only us though; almost everybody had that fear of their father. The question was always who would go and knock on the door, because we knew Dad always locked it. As soon as we knocked, he opened and invited us in, with that look in his eyes I always hated. We would be scared like hell and feel guilty that once again we betrayed him. He barely ever hit us, but we were so scared of him that one look from his eyes could ruin my whole day or night.

He would hold our hands tightly and say, "Didn't I tell you guys not to go outside?"

"Yes you did sir, but our whole world is outside, how can we listen to you?" is what we should have said, but who had the guts to tell him that? Khalil, my brother, was the goat, and I was the sheep. He would always jerk his hand away and run away, hiding, while I just stood there. I never understood why our Dad did that, really – to get us to beg for mercy, or to run and hide? I would do neither. He did not want to beat us, just to scare us. He would have to spank me or hit me to get me to say anything, then he'd let me go. Of course, the very next day, we were out with our friends again.

By the seventh grade my father had a lot more money. In Afghanistan people were not very business-minded. For instance, if my Mom had just kept twenty hens, a couple roosters, and raised chicks, she could have made twice as much as one did in a government job. My Dad made twice as much as my mother and even he could quit and make far more just doing private business. It was not only my Mom and Dad though, the majority of people didn't think about business, especially the city people. In fact, in Kabul, if your Dad was a barber, you could be teased at school, or if he was a baker, or a cook, or a shoe repairer, or a bus driver, or a shopkeeper. You could only be proud if you were a doctor, an engineer, an army officer, a professor, a teacher, a high-ranking government officer, or the owner of a big business, otherwise your children would be teased. That was one reason why everybody pushed their kids to go to university... to become a government officer. The pay was meagre, but it was prestigious! On top of his "prestigious" job though, my Dad would build a new house and sell our old one every so often, or just sell the new one (whichever made a higher profit) in order to bring in a few years worth of income in one fell swoop. But as this, again, had less prestige, it was merely a side job for him.

Building a house in Afghanistan was easy. My Dad always bought a larger lot, around a quarter of an acre, and then began constructing. While we were living in that house, he built a second one in the second half of the lot and sold it. You barely needed a permit to subdivide or a permit to build. It would only take him four months part time. All the houses were around the same neighbourhood, giving him far more money than his fellow soldiers. He also bought a two acre property in Jalalabad from the government for practically nothing, in a prime location, and that had appreciated in price almost fifty fold within couple years.

I was still a seven grader when my father was finally transferred back to Kabul, where we were living. He moved back in with us immediately. We kind of loved Dad, but we really didn't want to live with him. He made our lives so much harder. We lost a lot of our fun time. He wanted to jail us in our home. He only wanted us to go to school, do our homework, and make him tea. The other problem was that since he moved back in with us, Dad and Mom fought a lot more. My Mom did not have the concentration she had before because of the increased frequency. Dad, each time during the fight, warned Mom that he was going to marry another woman, and Mom always cursed him and told him to just do it "if he was a real man". At least a couple times a week these kinds of arguments broke out. The other problem was that since Dad had moved back in we had to leave one of the two bedrooms to him so he could have his privacy with Mom, and we were all stuck in the other room at night – all of us.

My father's threats of taking on a second wife became more and more frequent. As Dad was a bit richer than and not as busy as before, he had more time to visit his family and relatives around Kabul. His threats took on a greater sincerity over time as well. Eventually my mother stopped giving birth every two years, and an extra year passed by before the eighth child was born. During the pregnancy it looked like our parents had stopped much of their bickering. Mom also got into real estate a bit, buying a piece of property in Kabul at a huge government discount. Dad ended up getting her to sell it though, so they could paint the house and buy her a little jewellery.

Only a few weeks after the birth however, one of Dad's relatives came to us to tell us something that altered our lives forever – Dad he had indeed become engaged to another woman. The lady was half of Dad's age, and yes, we knew her. Her Dad was my Dad's uncle, and Dad was going to marry this guy's youngest daughter. Mom did not know what to do: to scream, to pull her hair out, to burn herself, to commit suicide, to kill her husband, or what. She felt completely and utterly betrayed. Dad had sold her building lot to paint the house because she was giving birth again, and he wanted to finally buy her a piece of jewellery, which he never bought her, and now he was actually using the money for the new wedding.

It was not just our Mom; all of us were doing miserably. Our whole world was shattered. We loved our Mom. To see her so devastated affected us very deeply. A few hours later Dad showed up from work, unaware that Mom already knew about the other woman. As soon as he got inside a fight broke out, and she began cursing him relentlessly. Dad, realizing that she knew, started getting very apologetic and kept saying, "I am sorry, mistakes happens, I did not want this, it just happened." He told Mom that he somehow got sexually involved with the girl, and had no choice but to get engaged. It was a big offence in Afghanistan to sleep with someone's daughter or sister without being engaged or married. You could be killed in a heartbeat. He needed to marry her before anyone found out. But for Mom, none of this mattered: she rather he was caught and killed for his offence, than to bring a second wife into her life.

In Afghanistan for a man to take a second wife, or even a third or a fourth, is not a problem. Usually women can't do anything about it, because Islam clearly allows men to marry four women at the same time. So if a woman fought against it, they could be labelled an infidel. That did not mean people accepted these laws, even if they had to follow them. It was most likely that Dad would kill our mother if she refused the situation, which is something no law in Afghanistan would frown upon. Still, she kept slapping Dad in the face and on the top of his balding head. He was not even defending himself. The group of us just watched as Mom kept slapping him and cursing – probably for ten to fifteen minutes, until she got tired. Soon as she had recovered though, she started up the beating again. The fighting continued all night.

The following day Dad did not return home. Now it was even harder for Mom. We did not have a phone to call around and find him. She sent every one of us to his relatives' homes to find him, to our aunts, our uncles, his cousins, just about everyone. Mom sent me to Paghman, my Dad's village. It was a gorgeous place, with nice weather in the summer because it was mountainous, and full of fruit trees. I always loved to go there, but it was nearly evening and there would be no way to get home later that night. Plus, I was so afraid of dark, that I always thought there were ghosts everywhere. When we were just children, our older siblings always scared us with tales of ghosts and Satan; scary stories. Sometimes adults, even your mother scared you off, just to make you obey them or listen to them, or to stop bothering them. I was so scared that oftentimes I was even afraid of my own shadow once the sun began to set. In my mind it was not a shadow, but a spectre. One time I ran a quarter of a mile from it; I thought one hundred thousand ghosts were chasing me.

The problem is that in Afghanistan, if you are a boy, it was a big embarrassment to be scaredy cat. So when my Mom told me to go to Paghman, that little village, to see if my Dad was there, I could not say that I was too scared to venture out on my own after dark. I could not tell my Mom that it was too late, and that by the time I got going to Paghman, it would be totally dark, and that I would be scared just being there period, let alone walking by myself for a mile or so along those dusty little winding roads, looking up at all those tall trees. When you are scared of dark, looking at trees is like being among two million phantoms, and when the wind blows even the sounds of leaves scare the hell out of you. But I could say nothing, lest I lose the respect of my siblings especially. They would no longer listen to me. I would no longer be able to act as an older brother to them, as their *Lala*.

I had to leave, and without any objections I did. Paghman was not that far, about 20 kilometres, but by Afghani standards it was a long way. First I needed to walk a couple kilometres to the bus stop, and then try to find a bus that went there. Then another walk to the few houses in search for Dad would be in order. I reached Dad's uncle's house around 10:30 pm. I knocked on the door as loudly as I could. The wooden doors were huge; like ten feet by eight feet and several inches thick.

It was a massive country home, with fifteen foot walls guarding the three-story fortress of a house. "Who is there?" the person inside asked, so with a loud voice I answered.

"Shafie, I am here for my Dad."

"Wait, I will be there in a moment."

Soon the door opened, and my step-mom's brother came outside with a light in his hand. He greeted me very kindly and invited me in, but it was with a cold voice that I thanked him. I wanted him to know we were hurt by what had happened. I asked him again about my Dad, and he said he was not at their house. "Are you guys hiding him?" I asked. But again, very politely, he said my Dad was not there. I didn't expect him to be nice to me anymore but still he insisted I come inside and have some food or tea. In Afghanistan people were very hospitable, they all wanted to share their food with you, especially in the rural areas. If someone was a close relative or even if someone was your bitter enemy, when they were at your doorstep you were really nice to them. This was the culture. It was unfortunate that Dad had gotten engaged with the guy's sister, but I was sure they were also unhappy and embarrassed.

When I was convinced father wasn't there, I turned around to go home. I changed my mind soon after though and went to go to the houses of my Dad's other relatives, another mile down to where the little road was even more dark and frightening. There was a two-story abandoned house along the way, like a witch's house. Even during the daytime our groups of cousins would run passed it. Now it is late at night, it was dark, and I was alone. I only made it half way before the fear took over again, and I couldn't go any further. As I turned to go back home the fear peaked. I couldn't shake the feeling that something unnatural was walking just behind me. I started to walk faster, then a little bit faster, and soon I was running as fast as I could. But the ghosts, they were as fast as me, and even started to come up beside me with their phantasmal, terrible forms. I was once again in a race with my shadow back to the bus stop. Damn shadow never seemed to get left behind!

When I finally reached the center of the little village there were a few lights and I felt better. I waited for a bus or a taxi going to Kote Sangi, the part of Kabul where we lived. While I was waiting for a ride though, I couldn't help thinking about what a wimp I'd been. But I couldn't keep myself from laughing at a certain point. It reminded me of another time I'd shown my yellow streak in front of my mother. She told me, "son there was a boy just like you, and he was petrified of the dark, even his own shadow. He was so scared of the dark that he bought a gun to protect himself. One night, as he woke up on the middle of the night, and as his eyes opened a little, he saw an ugly satanic face standing right in front of him. He very carefully picked up his loaded gun, aimed right at the head of the scary figure, and shot at it. The gunshot was then quickly followed by a great yelp coming from his very depths, as he realized the face was in fact his right foot resting over top of his left foot." His toes were gone. At least mine were still there! Thank god I did not have a gun.

It took an hour before a car came in my direction. I ran to the street and started jumping, waving at him. He did not stop initially, though you could tell he felt sorry for the little kid outside in the dark, and backed up his car. I moved forward and said hello to him. With a surprised voice he asked, "What are you up to in the middle of the night?" I told him that I was looking for my Dad, that we could not find him, and so I came all the way there to check his uncle's home. Now I was heading back home to Kabul.

He opened his door, and while he was driving asked my Dad's name. He recognized it. This was a small town; the locals all knew each other. He also knew my uncle and lots of my relatives. He brought me all the way to my house and I invited him in for a tea; he thanked me, declined, and went on his way. It was close to three in the morning. As soon as I knocked on the main door, my Mom opened it. Her worry had kept her awake all that time. She gave me a hug and kissed me, she was so happy to see me back. She did not even ask me about Dad, she was just busy telling me how happy she was that her son was back home.

My Mom, that great woman, was so different now. She was unhappy; so upset that she did not know what to do with herself. A couple days went by and Dad was still nowhere to be found. Soon Mom began to stir us up against him. She told us that he had abandoned us, that she was the only one we had. She told us that the only way to find him was at his work, and she wanted to put all of us in a taxi and take us to his office so his superior could see the kind of man he was. In the army, that would have ended his career. For my Dad that would be equal to cutting his throat. We knew what she was trying to do, even at that age.

The following day Mom put all the kids in a taxi, including the one month old, and took everybody to the military base. My older sister at that time was a twelfth grader and wanted nothing to do with it. My older brother also said no. So did I. The five younger ones had no option however, and were strapped in en route to the Ministry of Defence, as he had just been promoted to a position with central headquarters in Kabul. Mom could not care less; she wanted to embarrass him as much as she could. She saw her life ruined; she wanted him to suffer the same fate.

When they arrived there was a huge amount of shame poured upon him. Mom asked him for a divorce, but Dad refused. In Afghanistan, divorce was socially unacceptable and if your wife married another man it was almost like being labelled a pimp. Often the children were so embarrassed, that they would leave or even kill their mother to save face (not that this was on my mind, but it was the culture of the time). For a Mom with sons to go and remarry; she better be ready for all of this. My Dad had the law, the culture, the religion, and the people's minds on his side, while Mom had only the support of her children.

Dad was always using Islam in his arguments. Mom could not argue against that one, because her faith was just too deep, even if the Quran allowed men to take up to four wives. Dad kept quoting verses from the Quran and the story of the prophet Muhammad to support his "rights", and kept telling Mom that Muhammad, the prophet himself, had many wives. Mom just could not argue against that, even her own father had more than one wife – he had three. All she could say was, "But Muhammad was a fair man, he was dealing justice, and he treated all his women equally."

I was too little to really understand these kinds of conversations. I was trying really hard to digest all of the information. All I knew was I loved my Mom and that she was being victimized. I wanted to do something to help Mom but I was afraid of Dad. But more powerful than that was my love for my mother and my deep feelings of sympathy for her situation. What overwhelmed it all though, for the adults and the kids, for the married and the young, was our great fear of Islam. I was more afraid of Islam than the shadows in the woods. Although my mother knew that Dad had the right to have more than one wife and she very deeply believed in the same book that gave him that power, she fought very hard. But all of it was an uphill battle for mother. I did not see a happy ending for her in that war.

At times I believed my Mom was still lucky. I thought she still had a good husband. A lot of women did worse, and would have been lashed for even three sentences of what she had poured onto him over those days and nights. There were millions of women in that position not only in Afghanistan, but all over the Islamic world. My mother once told me about one of her friends, an army wife. We all knew each other. I was friends with her sons. Every winter when we went to Jalalabad we would see them, as they also wintered there. This army husband of hers, I remember his name was Wahid Khan, and he had two wives.

His wives were not fighting like my mother; they were living like they were slaves to their master. Mother told me that Wahid Khan's first wife found the second wife for him and she herself, along with Wahid Khan's sisters, went to the lady's family and asked her Dad to marry her daughter to Wahid. Everything went well and they got married. Only after the wedding did the new wife find out that the very same woman who had come to her house in order to propose was also the man's wife before her. Mom said that one day she asked Wahid Khan's older wife, who was Mom's friend, why she had arranged it herself. She told Mom that Wahid was making her life so miserable and beating her over and over again, demanding that she do it – that she find him a new wife. He beat her until she agreed. She could not complain anywhere, because the law was on her husband's side.

Now, when I looked at Wahid Khan and my Dad and compared them, well that comparison levied a lot of credit onto Dad. He put up with her pain, whereas a lot of other men would have simply killed her. It may be a harsh reality to hear, but it is how we lived. Looking back now, it often seems like even the best of men in that Afghani culture were still bastards. Despite all the fighting, Dad married the girl. He did everything in accordance to the laws of Islam now. He wanted to do exactly what the prophet himself had done: coming one night to our house to be with the older wife, and the next night he was going away to be with the new wife. But while it was easy for Mom to say "But the prophet was a fair man, he treated all his wives fairly and equally", in practice it did not make her feel better. She quickly understood that even doing it the prophet's way was not fair. Her faith in the value of what the book had to offer was beginning to peel away.

The arguments became a normal part of our lives, and Mom was not concentrating on the home and the kids like before. Sometimes she would not cook for days at a time. Sometimes she did not do the shopping on time and we would run out of things like sugar or cooking oil for even more days. I believe she felt that her husband's responsibility had disappeared, and saw her will to continue on with her own responsibility evaporating at the same rate. On top of this, I knew she wanted us to go after Dad and make him busier with ourselves, to cut his ties with the new wife as much as we could, but we were still scared of him.

My older sister escaped the situation by moving with my aunt. My older brother also went to my aunt's house and sometimes to the homes of other relatives. It was truly becoming a broken home. The rest of us were stuck with the trauma on a daily basis. I was the oldest of all that stayed home, and with the ebbing attention of our parents, slowly became in charge by default. The most embarrassing thing was that now their arguments were getting so loud that all our neighbours, even those a hundred feet away, could hear them. On top of that one of my classmates, and a close friend, was living one house away from us. He told the entire school. I was embarrassed as the neighbours began to find out some of the more sinister details of the whole charade... not only the neighbours, but my whole class room.

I no longer associated with a lot of my friends and became withdrawn within my own broken little world. As if my Dad had finally gotten what he'd always wanted. My grades improved substantially as a result, and as if at least one positive thing had to come of this all, within a year I became the top student in my class, and then my high school (one of the top most prestigious high schools in Kabul). My escape, instead of my friends in the street, became poetry. I began to read vociferously, classic Dari poetry became my closest companion. I fell in love with the words and can feel it filling in the empty spaces.

Soon my distraction became the distraction of my family, and my success became the focal point of the family in the community. That was exactly what I wanted. As I went deeper into the world of classical poetry I also discovered the philosophy behind the ancient poets. It was not merely a coincidence that many of those poets were followers of the same school of thought, geniuses all. I found out that almost all were Sufi, and that each became a proselytizer for the cause. They believed that all human beings were created by God, by the same God—all also agreed with the idea that man was raised up out of the dirt. They said that since God put his spirit within those people, and the spirit was a part of God, that the Holy Spirit was in everybody.

They concluded that all human beings were the same, regardless of the color of their skins, or their looks, or their gender, or their races or languages, or their wealth or their religions. We were all equal. The philosophy was responsible for saving millions of lives, especially since other than this one sect the majority of Muslims believed that if you were not a Muslim, you were *an enemy* of the prophet. Which meant we had a responsibility to wage Jihad against you. We invited you to become Muslims, but if you refused we would attack you, we would kill all the men and we would keep all your women for ourselves to be bought and sold as slaves in the market. Your kids could either be killed or kept as slaves as well – this is what we grew up believing, all of us.

It was this philosophy, Sufism, the philosophy of love and equality, which stood up against the brutality of many Islamic regimes. It was this Sufism that saved the lives of millions of Christians, Jews, Buddhists, Hindus, and even other Muslims. As I got deeper into the books I could see that the poetry was only the surface, that the colors bring you in, and that once you are there, thousands of doors open to you. Gradually you will be converted to a soldier of their ways of thinking. You will become one of them and they will teach you how to fight the extremists of Islam that always seem to come out of the darkness when no one's looking. Many times this philosophy reached up all the way into the smallest circles of power. But more than anything, this philosophy gave me something else to believe in other than the Quran, which always seemed to help Dad to do things I knew were wrong. He was right according to Sharia (the law of Islam), but not right according to the philosophy that gave great kings their truest understanding of the world around them.

26

The turmoil within my family pushed me out into these storms, into this tornado of ideals and cultural variances, into the middle of a Gobi desert of solitude. That poetry transformed my pain into experience. I started with Omar Khayam, then read Khajah Abdullah Ansari of Herat. I read them over and over until I heard the internal voice; until the whole book was memorized. I then read Hafez, Sanahi, Firdausi. Then a little Attar of Nishapur. Each one was a challenge for me to be able to read, let alone to understand. Each one of them was a pillar for a whole culture and language. It took me years, and then when I thought I was really ready, I came to Maulana Jalalludin Balkhi. This is where I was lost for years. That was totally different. You boiled, you burned, you were torn and shred into pieces and you disappeared into air, and then, you were reborn.

Maulana transforms you to a fish, to a swan, to a dove. With Maulana you find wings, and you can fly. Maulana, who was the most knowledgeable person about Islam, who had suddenly left his kingdom and become a Sufi, had fallen into an ocean of love and returned with his words to guide millions into his sea. But then, when I thought that was it, I found yet another book, another poet, another philosopher: Mirza Abdul-Qader Bedil. I then crossed the boundary of the Maulana planet to yet another world, even more beautiful, and they all, one by one, gradually took all my pains and frustrations and loneliness, and turned them to energy… an energy of love.

For the first two years Dad was with his second wife we did not see her, nor did we want to. Fierce arguments were a substantial part of our family life now. Off and on, Mom and Dad were fighting every day. Mom demanded a divorce every day, and father refused. Not that we would have wanted to see it go through either; that would have been too much for us to bear in a country where we would have been branded for life. Then early one morning when I was ready to leave for school, Mom asked me to come with her into the other room. She wanted to have a talk. I knew it had to be something incredibly important for her to speak in private.

"Son, listen carefully," she said, "Your Dad wants to bring his other wife to our house."

27

"To our house?" I exclaimed. I was shocked. Even at the time we first heard of the engagement I was not this shocked. "Mom, no, we will stand by you. We will not let it happen!" I said seeing the pain in her eyes. Mom was our leader. If we gave her a hand she could beat Dad, and we needed to. "So no, Mom, we are with you."

While I was refusing the idea, Mom was calm and quiet, which was unusual for her. "*Bachem* I already okayed it with Dad."

"What?" I was really shocked now. My mother, the same woman who had been fighting with Dad for the last two years over this issue, was now telling me that she already said yes to Dad to bring his second wife to our house?!? What in the world had this man has done to our Mom!?! Did he feed her some kind of pills or cast some kind of spell?

I knew why she was breaking the news to me first, as she was embarrassed to tell us all at once, plus she wanted to shut me up. "It's up to you Mom, but it's a bad idea."

"I know son, but your Dad is telling me that this woman is too young and he is afraid to leave her in a rental home by herself."

Now Mom was playing mind games with me. She could not wait to see Dad's second wife dead for years, but now she suddenly cared about her staying home alone? In Afghanistan it was a huge embarrassment if people talked about the women of your family, including your stepmother, in order to raise suspicions about their loyalty, morality, or ethics. In other word: she was trying to tell me that Dad was worried that she might have an affair. In that sentence I saw how much my mother loved the world, that she would not just rather see the woman killed for her eventual transgressions, and instead take her into her own home. But I knew it was, at that point, indeed a spell: a spell of words twisted by our father and levied upon her worried brow.

A week later a truck stopped in front of our house and we helped Dad to bring her belongings inside. We only had two bedrooms, when Dad was with us, one was his and Mom's, and the other was for all of us. Now what? After our stepmother moved into our house, in the evening my mother was with Dad one night, and stepmother was with him the other. The night my mother was not with Dad she slept with us, and Dad had the room to himself with his new wife.

But the night my mother was with Dad, our stepmother had no place to go, so she still slept in the room with the two of them.

I was amazed that at first things actually went well. There was about three weeks with no fighting. During this time Dad was doing just as Muhammad, our prophet, was doing: treating both wives equally. He was with the new wife one night and the other wife the following evening. But while he might have been quite satisfied, his wives were not. The peace lasted until the middle of the night, near the end of the month, when things absolutely exploded. Through the door of Dad's bedroom we could hear the triangle shouting and cursing each other. The argument kept us all awake, as we heard Mom and our stepmother cursing and beating each other, and our stepmother screaming "You cannot beat my husband anymore!" It worried us that much more that she was siding with Dad. We could tell that father was not intervening between the two of them.

We wanted to storm in and beat the hell out of this witch but Dad was there. Mom was a strong woman, but no match for her younger foe. The feeling of helplessness was corrosive to our souls. Even the neighbours were up from the racket. We had lived in that house for a long time. Our neighbours were like close family members. They worried so much, but had no idea what they could do to help. The women in the neighbourhood loved my mother. Especially the women whose husbands had more than one wife, who all stood firmly behind her. They did not know she had allowed this though, whatever her reasons. We had good support from the community, but boy this was embarrassing to me and my siblings.

The contrast between our dear, sweet mother and step mom couldn't be starker. While mother always ensured my older sister was safe from the parts of the world she knew were lying in wait for her outside that door, our stepmother would cuss her out nearly every day. As my sister would leave in the morning stepmother was just lying in wait for her, calling her names, telling her that for a young girl to go to school was as bad as moving to the city to become a streetwalker. The woman was illiterate, and whether she was proud of that or not, she was certainly trying her hardest to suppress the drive in my dear sister at every turn. She was now a university student in Kabul. The entire family was beaming with pride, so we found it very hard to swallow stepmother's words. This woman took our Dad from us, then moved to our house and took our bedroom, then started beating on our Mom, and now our sister. In Afghanistan calling a girl a hooker was like cutting her throat. We could each feel the blood of shame dripping down our necks. We consciously made things difficult for her, but were at the same time extremely respectful—and to be honest still so fearful—of Dad.

There were many examples of her vicious nature, leading to that inevitable day where everything came to a head. It was a Friday, around eleven o'clock, on a warm and sunny day. It the Friday that the washing was done and Mom was busy outside doing just that. My older sister was helping her and the younger siblings were helping too. My older brother Khalil and I were in the little back room we used for storage with our books open, but only pretending to do our homework. The truth was, I didn't want to go outside, because I didn't want to see my Dad or his new wife. Our hate for them had pushed us back into the corners of our little world. The patience in my little heart was ebbing every time I saw them. I remember, I leaned over to Khalil and looked him hard in the eyes. I told him, as I could feel my face becoming flush, that if this woman beat my mother again, I would beat her back.

"But Dad is there, our hands are tied," he replied.

"I don't care about Dad; I will stand up for Mom no matter what," I exclaimed in a firm, if juvenile, tone. And slowly it began to happen again… the arguments. Mother had sent one of my siblings to tell our stepmother to come and help her with the clothes as she also was a lady of the house. Suddenly out comes stepmother, cursing at the very thought of having to wash the clothes of another woman's children. My Mom cursed back at her. Then, as always, our stepmother leapt from behind her, blindsiding her with the attack. My pulse raced as the fighting erupted, and as if I had done it a thousand times before the adrenaline pushed me to jump outside. There before me was the image of our stepmother pulling Mom by her hair, dragging her along the ground. My older sister was trying to hold our stepmother's hands so that she would stop hurting my mother.

Like a wild dog I ran towards them. My hand raised, I put my fist into her face. In a flurry of rage I took her by the hair now and pulled her to the ground. My older brother was right behind me, kicking her, and then my Mom is up and beating her, my sister, all my siblings. Until now Dad had been neutral, just watching this woman beating my Mom, but suddenly now he had a soul and ran outside, shouting at us to stop. But as if we no longer knew him, and had simply become a mob of fierce justice, we continue to draw blood.

Dad quickly realized that we were not going to listen to him and ran to a nearby shovel. Picking it up in his hands, he went straight at my brother shouting, "Let her go!" My brother just ran, before father turned to me, holding the shovel up above his head and looking right at me. But instead of running, I looked him right back in the eye and began to shout, "Hit me! Hit me!" As if he could feel the rabid anger flowing through my veins into my eyes, his hands lost their power, and the shovel fell to the ground. The distraction was enough for our stepmother to struggle to her feet, her hair torn up and, like a witch beaten by the townsfolk, shrieking in pain she ran inside. Dad said not another word and followed her. There have been few moments in my life when I have felt such satisfaction. A clear message was sent by everyone in that home, that things were going to change.

The following morning once Dad had left for work, and Mom and the younger siblings had left, I, my older sister, and older brother, entered into our stepmother's room. Her demeanor had changed a great deal, as she sat there nervous, not knowing what would happen to her next. My sister started at her, "Why you are cursing me every morning when I leave to school? Do you really think going to school is equivalent to becoming a hooker?" I jumped at her and held her left hand as my older brother held her right. My sister wailed down her, slapping her over and over again. She slapped her as hard as she could, over and over again. Wilting, crumbling from her former violence, she began to cry for help, yelling and crying and begging for forgiveness. After a good beating we let her go, but issued a stern warning: "Make sure you leave this house, or you will be killed."

The following day father moved her out, and not once did we ever see her again.

Politics outside of the house were a furious in those days as the politics inside our home—there was a struggle in that part of the world over the way in which society should choose to move next. Communism was a big-time player in that argument. In the tenth grade though, busy with school, as any other tenth grader in that part of the world so close to the Evil Empire, I didn't know much about Communism. But there was a boy down the street from us about this time that had a book written by a man called Vladimir Lenin. He lent it to several boys, and eventually to me. What little I did know about Communism was in a historical context: I knew Lenin, I knew about the 1917 Marxist revolution that altered Russia forever, but it might as well have taken place on another planet as much as it affected our lives. He gave me another book after I read the first and I read that one too. I can't remember whether he didn't have any more or if it was that I simply lost interest, but my exposure to this idea had both begun and ended with skimming those two books just going around the neighborhood.

Winter eventually came as I finished the tenth grade. There is no school in the winter in Afghanistan, and the family would move to Jalalabad for the break where we had another house that was warmer in the face of the cold Afghan winters. Again, Jalalabad was like a heaven for us in those winters, where for three months we just enjoyed life and spent time with friends. But after Dad married his second wife, everything was turned upside down. We went two winters without returning: people would have died to have a house in Jalalabad for the winters, and we had one, but we never went anymore. I missed Jalalabad.

So I asked mother to allow me to go to Jalalabad with a close friend of mine, Samim. Samim's father was my Dad's friend, a math teacher at a women's high school. He had a private business on the side tutoring math and physics, and I had been taking lessons from him. That's how I met Samim. His Dad loved me like a son; I was his best student. While other teachers didn't want us speaking up, he would always laugh at the jokes I cracked in class. He would often invite me to his home and encourage my friendship with Samim. He knew of my family problems, and perhaps something in my resilience helped us form a bond.

Mom gave me the key to the winter house, and Samim and I left for Jalalabad. We reached Jalalabad around 11 o'clock - sunny, warm and gorgeous Jalalabad, my childhood heaven. Some of the most tender memories of my life were from there. I loved the people of Jalalabad, the trees of Jalalabad, the breeze, the vegetables, and especially the Nargis, a very fragrant lily. In the winter you could not see anything green in Kabul. In Jalalabad, life was still vibrant. The orange tree orchards were speckled with plump, fresh citrus and sugarcane popped up from the earth like sweet little soldiers.

From where the bus stopped in Jalalabad to our house was half an hour's walk. Samim and I, busy talking, moved toward our house. I remember the feeling of excitement as we got closer and closer. I remembered the first glimpse I got of it from the distance. I missed this place so much. My desire to kiss the house, the trees, the walls, the bushes, everything there, was strong.

One block from our house there was an old cemetery. Adjacent to the cemetery, kind of near the back side of it, there were some mud houses belonging to the locals. The people of Jalalabad were much poorer and less educated than in Kabul. Most of the kids didn't attend school (in this area they have winter school, getting summers off), so they all just played outside.

As we were walking, a Sikh man veered his bike right onto the unpaved road in front of us. The Sikhs were the only people of a truly visible alternate religion living in Afghanistan in those days. Although religiously life was really tough for them and discrimination ran deep, they had managed to live in Afghanistan for centuries. A little boy, about seven or eight years old, was riding on the front of the bike with him. As soon as he turned and got within a hundred feet of the cemetery, the local boys began to chase them, throwing stones from the ground – their turbans demarcated their difference in religion for all to see.

The man peddling the bike bent over the little one in order to protect him from the rocks and picked up speed. My temperature began to rise again, as I picked up a stone myself and raced after the boys harassing the poor Sikhs. My friend left his bag on the ground and followed me, as we chased the gang until they disappeared into their mud homes. The man on the bike turned back to stop and thank us. "You didn't have to do that," he said. He told us that it happened every day when he brought his son home from school. When I asked him why he did not complain to their parents he said, "I have done it many times but they never say a thing to their children." In Afghanistan, the Sikhs are considered lucky that they are at least allowed to live there with a special permission to practice their religion, as followers of any other religion do not receive this privilege. This is, of course, not an official permit from the government, but a permit from the people – the Sikh are tolerated, and the people largely turn a blind eye to their religious practices.

This was my second encounter of violent religion discrimination against the Sikh in Afghanistan. The first happened when I was eight or nine years old: I went to ShoorBazar (this old market in downtown Kabul) to buy a kite. Three Sikh women were walking in front of me when suddenly a gang of little boys attacked them the same way, throwing stones at them. The only thing these women were able to do was quicken their pace. They knew any other reaction could involve adults too; that they could even be killed. To this day I remember it as if it were happening right now. I always regret that I couldn't do anything at that time, though a small child has as little power there as they do here in America to comment on their surroundings in any meaningful way. When it happens, it just seems like there are so many others on the other side and just you and your little fists on the right one.

I need to say that in Afghanistan, and most of our Islamic societies, throwing stones at non-Muslims is seen as a blessing for some. We believe that as non- believers they will be sent to hell by God because they are dirty creatures, and if we punish them God will be more satisfied with us and will reward us in our next lives. We all believe that, but not all of us act upon that belief: something deep inside of us tells us not to do it. We may not say it publicly, but that is the way we think about Sikhs, Hindus, Christians, and all other kinds of non-believers. And to put it plainly, in Afghanistan, if you want to curse a Muslim, the worst thing is to call him – worse than the son of a donkey, worse than a prostitute – is a Jew. The Sikh were lucky that they had their own temples and could practice their religion, although privately and away from the eyes of the public.

34

When I was in high school a group of Christians, who were not even Afghan citizens and in the country as a part of a foreign diplomatic mission, somehow managed to get a permit from the Afghan government to build a Church there. As soon as the walls were raised, and the locals learned of their intentions, they rushed in protest and demolished it back into the ground.

The Sikh children, however, are allowed to go to school with us, but they are not allowed to stay in the class during our Quran and Islamic subject hours: we thought they were too unholy to be present when we read the Quran; this was the reason for many things that happen in our part of the world, not the least of which was the partitioning of Pakistan from India. It created many imbalances in our society. For example, I once had a Sikh classmate who was not able to score good enough at school to become one of the top students, only because he was not allowed to take the religious subjects tests (two of them) so his total points were always less than the rest of us, even though he was just as smart.

I am a Muslim, I love my religion, but I am always puzzled by this unfairness, which is something that first brought me to my love of poetry. These Sufi poets were the most humanitarian people in the Islamic world. They knew Muslims hated non-Muslims to the very depths of their souls in many instances and would kill non-Muslims everywhere without any hesitation. They wanted to prevent this, but were helpless themselves, and did not know how to enact change without provoking these Muslims to kill them too. They created instead a philosophy of love. If it was not for them, situations like the one with those three women would have been far worse.

By the twelfth grade things were better. Dad was coming home regularly, at least a few times a week—just like the prophet he wanted to be fair to both wives again. There was fighting, but not like before. I think Mom was a little tired of fighting now, and Dad already got what he wanted so there was no reason for him to fight at all. Dad had no control over us anymore though, he didn't need it. So I slowly became the head of the house.

By the twelfth grade I had begun to teach my classmates math and physics. A couple days a week I went one hour before the class started, and whoever needed help came in. I even helped the math teacher himself on occasion. When he had a question he would come to my classroom, knock on the door, and get permeation from my teacher to see me with his problem. This would bring me really close to a lot of people and I got their respect and trust.

During the two years between that winter in Jalalabad and now, I developed a different habit of sleeping. I went to sleep around ten at night, and then I woke up early in the morning and do all my readings and homework. My mind worked like an alarm. If I had enough to do, I would sometimes even wake up at two in the morning: right then. If five a m was required, I'd be up within a few minutes of that time too. Following my example, my brothers and sisters were doing equally well in school.

I helped them a little with their homework, but just them seeing me always at work and hearing good things about me from everybody pushed them in my direction. Our house was no longer a broken home, and respect came back to our family. Mom and Dad were happy for that, always secretly treating me, since financially they could not treat everyone in the family. At school I had made dozens of friends, each of them like brothers to me, all doing excellently in school as well. Samim and I still met up through tutoring with his father and outside of school too. Samim was still one of my close friends now. His Dad even stopped taking the fee from me while I continued to attend their private math and physics classes. In the high-schools the boys and girls go to separate schools, but in this private school we were together. That added to the pleasures of life. Not that anything was going on, it was that sitting next to them, talking to them, and to have the smell of them was so romantic. Believe me, in these Islamic counties, where girls and boys are separated, I can tell you the smell of a girl is so sexy – it draws you to them in a way you can't imagine in the West.

In grade twelve all students paid extra attention to their schoolwork, as the Concur tests were coming up. Thousands of students, all over Afghanistan, take this test on the same day. Based on the score of this test and making it their first choice, they have the opportunity to be selected for Kabul University. Out of the tens of thousands of kids that graduate from high-schools in Afghanistan, only a small portion had the chance to be accepted to the University. For

36

example, the medical Faculty could accept only about 250 students from perhaps ten thousand graduates who wrote down their first choice of program as Medicine; a few hundred got into Engineering.

In Afghanistan almost everybody wants their children to become doctors, because of the income and the prestige. My Mom and especially my older sister were begging me to choose Medicine as my first option, but I had no interest in it. I wanted something to keep me closer to the great writers I loved, and to help me develop that side of my heart. But my Mom and older sister finally forced my hand, and I put it as my first choice.

In 1978 I was selected as a medical student at Kabul University. Almost all of my friends also succeeded and they joined me there. One was with me in Medicine, a few in engineering, and a lot more in the other faculties. School and university were free and paid by government in Afghanistan. Our classes started around eight in the morning and went until twelve, when we would break for lunch and then class would continue into the afternoon. Almost all of my friends would gather at a designated place before lunch and then all go to lunch together at the university cafeteria, which was also subsidized by the government and sold us lunch cheap enough that we could afford to eat.

We were perhaps the biggest group walking to the cafeteria together. Even when we went to the library or to the private tea house Chay Khana, we always went together. These times were filled with joy. I laughed a lot with my friends. We were very close: if I said we would have died for one other, I wouldn't be lying. Khalil, my brother, was in the engineering faculty, he was also a part of our group. I guess I was finally "cool" enough for him to hang out with. Every Friday we would go to a movie or a friend would invite us for tea or dinner.

I began to know the families of my friends, even their sisters. In Afghanistan there is this distinct and clear boundary for social relationships. You can barely get as close to some to say hello to their sisters let alone talk to them. And when you do, it is your responsibility to keep everything clean. You cannot even think about having a relationship, or romance to one of your close friend's sisters. You cannot even think about getting married to one, because you don't want your friends to think that your friendship with him was not pure and you had his sister in mind. Afghans are very sensitive about their women. You better stay away, or you must be as clean as possible. Don't get me wrong, sometimes it happens that people marry their friend's sisters, or two friends each other's sisters, but this truly is not common.

At university, now for the first time, we are with the girls, studying together. It's another audition for us. We began to talk more about girls, tease with them when they pass, or try to say something sweet to them. It is the beginning of a new chapter in our lives.

Then, in only our second month at the university, a military coup toppled the government. The monarchy that had ruled over Afghanistan for over half a century was thrown out. A government that we blamed every one of our country's problems: the slow economic growth, illiteracy, and broken financial infrastructure. The people hated the monarchy so much that even if we got too much rain we would blame them for it; or an earthquake; or a drought. The King, who called himself the first elected President, had in fact toppled his cousin Muhammad Zaher Shah through coup himself while he was visiting Italy approximately four years before that. Mohamad Daoud sponsored a Loya Jirga, bribing thousands of elders, and used them to install himself as an elected President. Although he was much better than his cousin, and was doing more for our country than his cousin had before him, the majority of the people still felt in no way connected to the government. So although people still didn't know much about the coup and who was in charge of it, nobody was upset about the fact the monarchy was gone. In fact, for a lot of people, especially for the educated, it was welcome news.

On the way home there were military tanks everywhere. Some news spread later in the day that Daoud Khan, the President, was either dead or behind bars. The coup was unlike the coup from four years ago. That one was a bloodless coup, but this one had its fair share of executions. Not a single shot was fired in the prior event, but this time the tanks and heavy artillery sounds were everywhere. Even more of the heavy sounds were heard from where the Presidential palace was. Sometime later in the day, military jets hovered in the sky and I could not tell if they were attacking the palace where the King was, or they were pro-government and attacking the anti-government forces. We had no TV in the country, but soon Radio Kabul, which was temporarily disturbed from their programs, started up again and announced the end of the one-family government era: the era of Ahl-e-Yahya.

Still, we were curious as to who was in charge of the coup; rumor had it that it was simply the military itself. Later, some leaders belonging to a Communist group (the Khalq and Parchan wings of the pro-Soviet communist party) announced through the government radio channel that they were the ones to end this one-family rule. They announced a new beginning for our country and our people: the government of the people, by the people, for the people. I remember that we were all happy. People were congratulating each other. Some were sad about Daoud's family, who were killed during the coup, but other than that the vast majority of people were happy.

Many people at that time were not familiar with the ideology of Communism, even the educated people. We knew that there was the Communist Republic of China and the Soviet Union, and that they were communists, but only a small percentage of people really, really knew what that meant, or much about the Soviet Union, and about this Afghan communist organization now in charge. The amazing thing was that a majority of the leaders of these communist organizations had been arrested a week ago.

There were rumors that the President/King wanted to eliminate them soon, to get rid of the threat they posed. Four or five years ago the newly ousted President Muhammad Daoud was closely connected to this same communist party and, in fact, used them to topple his cousin Muhammad Zaher Shah. Then, after he got the power he wanted, he pushed his previous friends and allies away. The Communists finally got upset and started to plan to incite people against the Daoud. He arrested all the leaders, and wanted quick executions, but with help from Russian embassy and the pro-Soviet Afghan officers in the army, which had some important positions, the communists quickly toppled the Daoud regime in response.

I was only an eighth grader when Daoud Khan toppled his cousin. Daoud Khan then quickly banned all the political organizations, making them illegal. Just four years ago, before King Zaher was toppled by his cousin, having a political organization or demonstrations, or having anti-government newspapers, was not something openly oppressed by the government. There were many political organizations active in Kabul. None of these organizations really had their own ideas for Afghanistan though, they were followers of some outside ideology, and most of them were getting some financial and material support from outside the country as well.

Even when we were in the fifth and sixth grade, sometimes the demonstrators from the high-schools or Kabul University came to our elementary school, forcing the doors open and asking us to come with them. We were too young to understand that these marches were in protest of the King, but we loved the early dismissals. I remember from those demonstrations, there were these Islamist extremists, but most of us were not fans of them. In Afghanistan at that time, especially in Kabul, people were not excited about them at all. Most of them had these long beards, some were not even dressed properly, they wore their robes and turbans in funny ways, reading verses of the Quran. We were all Muslims and very respectful and fearful of our religion, but we were not fan of these people, they were too extreme for the mentality of the Kabul people.

We also did not like them, because they were so restrictive and mean. We came to hate them even more, as they became known for spraying school girls with acidic chemicals to discourage them from putting on skirts or even going to school. The younger ones in the Muslim extremist group (Ikhwanis) were mostly kids from rural areas living in dorm and the Kabul kids did not like them much. People in Kabul were not dressing like them, not thinking like them, and did not want to associate with them. Even girls did not like them; in Kabul girls did not want to marry those bearded men, who were so restrictive, not even allowing their wives to work.

That didn't mean they did not have any followers: there were still enough people to make them one of the top four organizations at that time. It did not mean that we were never doing what most of them told us to do, because we were in line with that too. The rule in those early days as a grade-schooler was that whoever came first and opened our school doors, we would go with them. Then we would follow them all the way to downtown Kabul, to a designated area for demonstrations, called Park-e-Zarnegar, one of the two famous parks in Kabul. My classmates and I would stand with them for a while and listen to their lectures, then we would walk over to another gathering belonging, for instance, the pro-Soviet communist party of Khalq, then to the next gathering of Parcham (another pro-Soviet party), and to the next one which was a pro-Chinese Maoist party, Shula-e- Jaweed. There were a few smaller ones too.

Our purpose at that time was not to be real anti-government demonstrators, we just wanted to enjoy our early dismissals, but at the same time we were kind of listening to these leaders and trying to understand. They were all talking against the government, which was easier for me to understand, but most of the time they were talking against the other anti-government movements. In fact, they spoke more ill of their competitors than anybody else, and I was always confused about why they did not simply join forces if they were so against the autocracy. Even the Khalqis and Parchamis, who were both communists and both pro-Soviet, were each other's enemies. Being a communist at that time was quite fashionable. You could impress people by telling them that you cared about the poor and you want equality, it was something people did to fit in. I remember everything, and I know now how much freedom we had. But still we were calling King Zaher a dictator.

I was only in the eighth grade when Daoud toppled his cousin King Zaher and banned all the political organizations, their newspapers, and any kind of demonstration. Even at that age we did not like it, because there would no longer be those early dismissals! Banning these political organizations was a huge blow to all of them, because as they did not have any clear manifesto, and any organized or accepted ideology, or any practical working programs, they had no means to survive without publicity. Many just shuttered and turned to small private talking parties, and the rivalry even between these private groups got even worse, making it even harder for them to exist; like an infectious disease the rivalries started to choke each other out.

Among the pro-Soviet communist parties, the Khalq and the Parcham were able to stay alive and continue their work underground, as they had continued (if not increasing) financial and political support from the Soviet bloc and also had ties with President Daoud himself, until (of course) things got sour and Daoud put all of them in jail. An action that ensured that he and his entire family, except (I believe) for one of his sons, were dead by the following morning.

This swath of new lethal power alarmed the other political organizations, from the Maoists to the Islam extremists, but we, the regular people of Afghanistan, welcomed the change. We believed that this was going to be a positive change; we had faith in our country. Everywhere people were giving flowers to the army officers patrolling the streets. People were dancing, singing, and partying.

For me, this was welcome news. I hated the one-family government. I was so excited that I wrote a poem in ode of the event, which I read to my class the following morning at university. People seemed surprised – they did not know I was a poet.

Only a few weeks into the life of this new government though, we were very aware that it too in no way belonged to the people. And on top of it all we were caught by the worst surprise of our lives. Like animals with an appetite that cannot be tamed, the new government formed a secret police force within the members of the party, who wasted no time before they rushed into the residences and workplaces of anyone they remembered from the demonstrations from five years ago, disappearing them forever. And in no way did they allow anyone to complain about the arrests.

Five years prior I remembered that the leaders of this same communist party were blaming King Zaher for not giving people enough freedom of speech, but in those days people were allowed to proceed with all kinds of demonstrations against the government. They were allowed to have newspapers and all kinds of other freedoms, but now they were arresting people themselves by the tens of thousands, slaughtering them in most cases, and nobody was allowed to say a word.

If a mother complained about the disappearance of her teenage son she could go to jail too. The blue sky over Kabul turned dark:

it was fear that governed now, with no escape. The only people that had the connections to get out of Afghanistan were the Muslim extremists. Many escaped to Pakistan, but the majority of people belonging to the other political groups were jailed or killed – often jailed and then killed. The happiness and those flowers in the hands of the soldiers, and the singing and the dancing and those poetry readings turned to fear and tears and worrisome days.

Everybody was asking, "When is my turn coming, or my Dad's, or brother's, or uncle's, or friend's, or neighbor's turn coming?" It was not only the political rivals that they were after; they also quite happily put you in jail just because you were rich. In Afghanistan even the rich are poor, but for these communists, if you had more than you could eat, you were rich; you belonged to bourgeoisie, and the bourgeoisie were against the labor's interest, thus you were eliminated. If you had a car, you were too rich. If you had enough money to paint your house, you were too rich. If you had more than one house, you were too rich. The problem was that these communists were communists just to look good, and the majority did not even know what Communism was. They just memorized a few highlights from communist writings, and transferred their pro-Islamic prejudices to pro-communist prejudice.

The two communist parties, the Parcham was filled with mostly city people, and the Khalq were rural people. For this second party, even if you had new clothing you were considered an anti-revolutionary and could be captured and killed. A lot of the members of this group were anti-city people and, just like the Taliban, they did not understand the Kabul lifestyle in their villages, giving them another reason to send people to jail. They were not prosecuting anyone, there were no laws, or rules, or courts, or judges. If you were caught by them there was only a minimum chance that you would be released.

Even from our class itself they captured several seventeen or eighteen year olds, within the first few weeks. They were arrested and never seen again. Soon people were extremely cautious of saying even a word against the government. In the same neighborhood where my family and I were living, there was another family that suffered a fate we came to fear. They lived a mile further down

43

from our home and most of the time, when we were playing out-side, we would see them walking. Their next door neighbors were a family closely related to Noor Muhammad Turaky, one of the com-munist party leaders, and the current President of Afghanistan. That family next to this Turaky's relatives suddenly disappeared, all of them, forever. They were all arrested and killed, because one of their little kids tore up a newspaper one day that had Turaky's picture on the front cover.

What was saving me from death, besides God, was that little poem I read to my class when the communists took over. In our class there were about four members of the Khalq wing of the commu-nists and they thought that I was a Khalqi. Especially as one of the most powerful leaders of Khalq, in fact the most powerful leader, Hafizullah Amin, was from Paghman, and so was I. They thought we were related—it was the most random acts and instances that kept me from being disappeared myself. I was, in fact, the perfect target for their crazy paranoia to come down upon. Pacha Gul, the head of the medical faculty communist youth association, was our class-mate. Several times he told me that they were getting bad reports about me, but he was defending me, saying that I was their friend. I was one of the people who truly hated what had happened to our country, so it was a swift kick to my soul to hear him defending me, calling me a friend. But thank God he was there.

Only a couple months from the time the coup succeeded, something inside of me urged me to do something about all this. Something was pushing me, something was urging me, to stand up for my people. I already did things for my family, for my siblings, for my Mom, but now I felt the need to provide for my helpless people. So one day at the end of summer I invited about twenty of my friends for a meeting and asked them to form a student orga-nization at Kabul University, creating some kind of resistance to the brutality of this new government. We were the most important part of this governed body, I told them. We were educated, we were young, and we had people at university from all parts of our country. We could at least publish some anti-government pamphlets, secretly distribute them, and gradually unify our people against this govern-ment. There were about twenty people at that meeting, and they all agreed with me. We knew it would be a difficult task, being caught meant death. But we started, by inviting our close friends, whom we'd known for a long time, to join us. Soon we were few hundred people strong: the "Kabul University Revolutionary Youth."

As one might imagine, it was inevitable before the old frictions between the two communist parties resumed on the ground. No matter how well-oiled their coup and the aftermath may have been, the old disagreements stemming way back to the protests on the square reared their heads again. The result spread into the upper ranks and as the Khalq party had more members in the army, they were able to subdue the Parcham leaders, putting them in unofficial exile as ambassadors to the Soviet bloc countries or, in the case of the famous Parchami Dr. Najibulah, to Iran.

It created a very uneasy situation inside the entirety of the party, and that uneasiness itself turned into significant turmoil moving in the direction of full scale civil war. Of course, for the regular people of Afghanistan this is a brief bit of respite, as the busier they were fighting each other, the less they focused on killing ordinary Afghans. The members of the Khalq wing of the communist party were mostly Pashtuns from rural parts of Afghanistan. They were, on the most part, educated, determined, and loyal; and resembled very much the rural Taliban of modern times. They were extremists, brutal of mind and in action, with a titanic chip on their shoulder against urban dwellers.

Key members were extraordinarily racist against non-Pashtuns. The Parcham wing members, mostly city people, were also all educated, just as determined, but a little less brutal, were a mix of Tajiks, Hazara, Uzbek, and Pashtuns. The Pashtuns in the Parcham were largely urban dwellers, thus much less loyal to their particular ethnic backgrounds. They considered themselves Afghans first, and this cultural difference between the two wings was palpable, breaking apart the glue that Communism had provided them to paste themselves together.

At the top of the Khalqi wing of the communist party was the old man Turaky, who was at most points interested in trying to work with the Parcham, but the real power was in the hands of Khalq's second in command: Hafizullah Amin. He was the one who truly sought to subdue the world around him. Amin was an excellent speaker, active within society and very charismatic. He was in fact the only key leader of the communists to escape arrest by Daoud Khan, and while all the other leaders were in jail he single-handedly managed the coup against Daoud from hiding, toppled the government of an entire nation, and freed all the communist leaders from jail. Hafizullah Amin was the center of power while Turaky sat as a spiritual figurehead overtop of it all - even Amin kissed his hands whenever greeting him. The scene of Amin kissing the hands of Turaky was a common one in those days, especially on the single public television channel where Amin famously referred to Turaky as *Ustad-e- Buzurg* (my great teacher/leader). That was a lot for a man like Hafizullah Amin to say.

Turaky, however, would not fall into line with the focus on solitary power that Amin had established, something Amin would quickly learn. On a trip to Havana in order to meet with other leaders from the Soviet bloc, Turaky had alongside him one of Amin's most loyal friends. In the Cuban sun the dictators and their inner-circles no doubt discussed things such as world domination and the destruction of their enemies at length. Over long Churchill cigars they would have ironically discussed the core principles of their common movement, despite the tremendous gaps between their home cultures.

On the way back from the conference, Turaky and his party made a stopover in Moscow in order to meet with President Brezhnev of Russia. There, in no doubt a push to establish firm Soviet bloc control and stable Communism in Afghanistan, Brezhnev pushed Turaky even harder to unify the two wings of the communist party and keep them together. Whether or not Turaky had believed so before the meeting, afterwards he was fully convinced that the only benefits of internal conflict would go to the anti-government forces.

To unify the two wings of the communist party, Turaky knew that Hafizullah Amin was on the way, so he had to agree to a plan with the Amin's enemies - the Parcham wing leaders, now in exile. As soon as Turaky got back to Kabul, the plan was discovered by Hafizullah Amin. For Amin to see his own so-called leader betray him was something he could not take. He immediately sought ways to remove Turaky altogether. The final straw for Amin was the rumor that Amin's own assassination was in the works. Amin moved immediately and arrested Turaky at the presidential palace. He then ordered two of his non-communist guards to suffocate his great teacher. Turaky begged and pleaded with them to bring Amin to him just once, so that he could convey something of the utmost importance. But Amin, true to his nature, refused to hear his mentor's last words.

The guards placed a pillow over Turaky's mouth in September of 1979 and pushed down as hard as they could, until the last futile movements of his limbs had shaken free and he had been eliminated from the situation. For several days the death was kept a secret, until Amin announce his death from a "health issue". The Afghan people erupted in happiness once again, waiting in anticipation for the entire government infrastructure to just slit each other's throats. The rumor that Turaky had been assassinated spread even more joy. Anti-communist jokes were made instead of any kind of mourning. A jubilation that served to largely cover up a growing fear that if Turaky wasn't safe from Amin – who was?

Amin soon learned though that he needed to make peace with somebody, as his enemies were multiplying by the day. In an act of true cowardice, Amin decided to come out against the slaughter of innocent Afghans, who had died by the tens of thousands, blaming it all on Turaky. He pledged both to put an end to the actions and promised the people that he would provide a list of all the prisoners—and what had happened to them after their arrest. Soon enough a list was hung with the names of over twenty thousand innocent Afghans each shot dead; in the stark desert sun at a place they called Polygon Field.

Yet tens of thousands of others were still missing, with no word from the government. Rumors spread once again, that those not registered as deceased by the government had been sent to Siberia, where they were being forced to work in Russian labor camps. All the joy had left the streets of Kabul. Even that jaded joy that crept up inside of the fearful had been suffocated now, as all hope of seeing the missing again was plucked from the souls of the people. After all this, the people were still not buying Amin's story - they knew that as the most powerful leader in the party nothing could have happened without his say-so. The arrests were only reduced temporarily, though the announcement of government executions remained the norm from that point forward. Afghans were still dying, but their names were now written on a piece of paper – what significant progress, don't you think?

The killing of Turaky was seen by the Russians as undermining the power and authority of the KGB. It was like a slap in the face of President Brezhnev, who had developed a relationship with Turaky. Amin had now made an enemy much more powerful, and much more terrifying than any secret political organization on the domestic front. The order to get rid of this mad man, Hafizullah Amin, came from Brezhnev himself. And Amin was simply not smart enough to see it coming, believing instead that now that all his domestic competition has been trampled, the Soviets had no choice but to work with him.

Things were falling apart as the citizenry began to strike back at the communists, much the same as our dear family struck back against our evil stepmother. Attacks on the communist party members in their homes, on their way to work, in their cars, and all other places became more common. The people confiscated their weapons and began hunting them down, using their own weapons against them in the killings. The Parcham rose up once again against Hafizullah Amin, and were now in bed with the followers of Turaky who saw Amin's assassination as an act of treason. Volunteers, eager to exact revenge on behalf of their fallen loved ones, began to populate spreading resistance groups.

My own student organization had grown into a substantial and active one by this point. Once a year had passed, and we had enlisted more than one thousand members. We were successful in publishing several anti-government newsletters, and managed to distribute them around the university without getting caught. It might not sound like a lot, but they were short little steps that led to progressively longer strides. As the Afghan resistance grew bolder, the world's attention became focused on the affairs of Afghanistan and help began to arrive through Pakistan. However, as it has been with all twists and turns in recent Afghan history, this event had its darker underside. Until then, Islamic extremists were not a major factor in the war against Communism in Afghanistan. With tens of millions of dollars being poured in Pakistan, a new era began. The war, which had its nests in Afghanistan and the common folk, was increasingly dominated by Pakistan-based radical groups and the struggle was proclaimed an Islamic holy war: a Jihad.

The Soviets watched and waited as the division between the pro-Soviet communists in Afghanistan grew, and as the common people's resistance merited more and more international attention. The plan to eliminate Hafizullah Amin and unify the entire Soviet-style side of the government into one organization was put into action. The KGB convinced Amin, soon, that the situation was kind of getting out of hand. They drove Amin's paranoia about an uprising that could steal his power, persuading him that the best solution would be to allow the USSR to send in the Red Army to protect Amin's regime.

In the winter of 1979, the sky over Kabul was now altered forever. A rumbling was heard from afar, as if a great beast had awoken. Like a dark cloud of hornets, a swarm of huge military airplanes blotted out the sun. On board were equipment, soldiers, and the weapons of regime change. I remember huddling around the radio secretly listening to the BBC as they announced the movement of Soviet tanks and even more soldiers crossing the land border. Nervousness does not nearly describe how we felt that night. Until then at least the murderers were Afghan communists. Now, foreign troops had directly invaded our country.

In my lifetime, and at least for over half a century, no foreign soldier had set foot in our lands. Rich or poor, we were at least a free people. Every step those soldiers took into our world cut a little deeper into our pride and our sense of security. Most of all we were afraid of the rumors that the Soviet troops came looking for local women in their downtime, with a thirst for flesh that haunted every footprint left behind them. An Afghan would easily sacrifice their life to prevent anything like this from happening, even more than they would to preserve the sanctity of Islam. Instead of dampening the uprising, the arrival of the Red Army motivated swaths of more people to join the anti-government movement, even to cooperate with the extremists coming in from Pakistan that everybody hated.

These cancerous cells of extremism began to grow, taking advantage of the pain and suffering in our country, in malignant silence behind the scenes. Nobody was asking questions about the integrity of these Islamic organizations; just to be against the government was enough.

Within a week there were hundreds of Soviet Tanks in Kabul. Then, it finally happened. I remember about this time sitting at one of my close friend's houses, a couple miles away. Their house was on a major road that connected Kabul to the military base Qargha. Close to 10pm a long line of military tanks started to pass along the road, heading from Qargha towards the new presidential palace, where Amin then resided. Every tank had Soviet markings on them; there were no Afghan tanks. Staring at this line of iron giants, I knew deep down that something was very wrong.

Within a few hours the sounds of an intense military struggle could be heard coming from the direction of the palace. Everybody was awake now, each of us sitting in front of our radios waiting for word as to what was going on – and, for those of us who saw the tanks, who the victors would be. Soon, a familiar voice: Babrak Carmal, the leader of the Parcham party. He had been sent into exile by Amin one and half years ago, and was the man with whom Turaky hoped to negotiate away the divisions within the communist party. Plucked out of his Soviet hideout, he had been sent back by the KGB to become the new leader of our Afghanistan. His voice was shaky. You could tell that he was reading from a piece of paper that had just been handed to him, or from a long rehearsed speech meant to hide the reality of what was truly going on. Soon enough it was discovered that Carmal had not been in Kabul that night, but rather in Tajikistan, with his voice broadcast and relayed from Radio Tajikistan.

Amin was dead, and yet another leader stood before us with promises of being a moderate and stopping the disappearings. He announced the release of all political prisoners, and promised a better life for the people. But for Afghans, it was too little, too late. For Afghans, he was a treasonous man who allowed foreign occupation, and the anti-communist resistance simply continued.

Our student association continued to grow, with branches in all the Kabul high-schools. Professors began to join our ranks, as did the high-school teachers. Our little newsletter was called the *Shabnama*, and its distribution continued unabated. Ashraf, one of our members, had access to some typewriters: he was the one who typed up all of our pamphlets. In order to speed up the dissemination, he would place carbon paper between the sheets to get more copies out of one typing job, and would sit there for days at a time just typing copy after copy after copy. This carried on until the day we finally gained a member whose family friend had hidden some of his publishing equipment away after the new regime made publishing an illegal enterprise (all presses were shut down), and volunteered to print our pamphlets from then on: a man named Muhinauldeen.

I was so grateful to Ashraf and Muhinauldeen, who would take the pamphlets I wrote in entirety and turn them into a public work, working directly with me day after day. Our ranks grew to 2500 very active members, and we were pretty much in charge of Kabul University and the surrounding high-schools. The *Shabnama* became more regular, and more influential as time went on, as Kabul began to boil over with anger. In February of 1980, just two months after the invasion of Afghanistan, the people stormed the streets in an anti-government demonstration. At first the government tried to play nice. Soon though, armed soldiers rushed into the streets with guns blazing. Hundreds lost their lives in couple of hours, as the soldiers shot indiscriminately. I remember instructing my brothers and sisters to stay inside and not march that day, as the reaction to the protests had become as vicious as the protests themselves. Having us die in the streets in front of a line of soldiers that were as terrified as we were would not help our country, I said to them. Our goal was not to kill ourselves, I said. They agreed.

The night before those protests though, I was at a friend's house. In the early morning I was walking home when I saw a few buses packed with a couple hundred people(all Hazara) in Kote Sangi, the center of the city where we were living at the time. As soon as they got off the bus they began chanting anti-government slogans and rhythms. The group drew bystanders to them like a magnet, and in the blink of an eye the group became thousands strong. Their direction was the Kote Sangi police station, which just happened to be the direction I was walking in. Our house was quite close to this police station.

As I was walking I looked over to see my two younger brothers shouting anti-government slogans in the crowd. I picked up my pace, walking faster to reach them, shouting, "Why are you here!" Once I had caught up with them we had no choice, were now a part of the mob, and my goal was just to get as close to home as possible so that we could get out of the situation. Suddenly the demonstrators turned one street east of the main road that had the police station. We were again being swept along in the direction of our home, so close to freedom yet, in tandem, so close to a place I knew we truly did not want to be.

A mile further they turned right, only a couple of blocks from the station. We have managed to stay out of the thick of it, at the end of a huge line of demonstrators which is about a quarter mile long. As they reached that main road they made another right, and started marching towards their target. By the time we reached the main road ourselves, the front end of the march was within a block of the police station. I knew that we just needed to walk across the street at this point, and that then we could walk home without going anywhere near the danger up ahead.

Gunfire erupted. The police opened up on the crowd. People were lying on the ground, diving to get out of the way of the bullets. We didn't even have a chance to move across the main road, only sixty feet wide. A wave of people forced us backwards, pushing us back to the road that we had just come from. A chaotic mess of humanity took shelter in the houses, some jumping into the stores. But after the pushback, much of the crowd began to chant, "*Alahu Akbar, Alahu Akbar!*" People, excited again, pushed forward, and again shots rang out into the crowd.

To my right there is a teenager that I know lives right at that corner where we are stuck. As we try to cross the road and run towards our home, his little arm is raised with a stick in his hand, shouting with the crowd "*Alahu Akbar, Alahu Akbar,*" and moving alongside the demonstrators. For the third time the police start shooting. The boy collapses. Rushing to his side, I could see the bullet hole bubbling blood inside his mouth – his anger, and his future, plucked directly from his vocal cords. My brothers and I begin to drag him out of the street, his dead body mere feet from the home where he would have laid his head to rest the night before. Within moments, his cousins realizes what happened and comes flying out of the crowd, taking his body from us and bringing it into the house.

After that, except for the bodies of dead, the main road was empty. My brothers and I hide by the corner, waiting for a chance to run to the other side of the road. But every time someone goes to jut across the road, the police start to shoot again. At a certain point I realize that in my hand was the stick of the boy who was shot beside us, I must have unconsciously took it with me. I held it in my hand as if it were a sacred flag, a symbol I did not want to be left on the ground. It resembled the size of a baseball bat, and I imagined at the time what he might have done with it if he had gotten a hold of one of those traitorous Soviet sympathizers.

The military planes soon arrive above the street breaking the humble silence, and the sky is filled with roars. When they had first come into Kabul their noise represented that feeling of invasiveness that we each felt that week, but they were now flying so low that we needed to plug our ears in order to not have them ring once the behemoths had passed. It was as if a great ogre was leaning down over us, growling and breathing heavily just to let us know it's there. I take a deep breath and grab both my brothers close to me. I look at where I want to go and envision myself on the other side. And with a burst of energy, I run full speed, dragging my brothers with me, into the street…

A few minutes later we reached home. It was Friday, wash day, again. As we entered the yard though, I saw Mom, just sitting there. The clothes were in the middle of being washed, but she had withdrawn from the task as if it no longer mattered. The sight of that bloody baseball stick in my hands shook her free of waiting. "What is that?" she cried. As I told her the story, I could see my sisters lift their hands to their eyes, trying to hide the onrush of tears.

Nobody ate that day. When the police finally allowed people to collect their dead, dozens of bodies were gathered from the street and placed in our street mosque. And this was only at our single neighborhood mosque – the same thing was happening all over Kabul, at hundreds of different mosques. One by one, families came to see if they had lost someone. It was the biggest uprising to that date against the Soviet invasion. Tens of thousands of people participated all over Kabul. Hundreds were killed. They named it the *Qyam Soum Hoot*.

Two months we were on the verge of another massive demonstration, but this time it was the university students who wanted organize the anti-government demonstration. During the last one I had told my two younger brothers not to participate, advice they did not listen to at the peril of death. But this time I had a responsibility not just as an older brother, but as the head of the Kabul University student association that had been one of the seeds of the very resistance that soaked our streets with blood. I knew that I needed to make sure that history did not repeat itself.

We already knew what the government reaction would be the moment the demonstration arose. The secret service could easily identify all the organizers, and the most active people. We wanted them to be able to remain active for as long as possible, and if they were killed or arrested, the blow for the university and the people in general would be grave. We had some reports the following morning that some of the students had planned to start the march; most of them were engineering students. Our organization knew it had to do something, but when we tried to get in touch with somebody we quickly realized that there was no particular organization in charge of the push to speak with.

I urgently wrote a pamphlet to distribute the following morning encouraging stufents to stay away from the demonstration, as we knew the government would use it to their own advantage. But just as my little brothers were swept up in the fervor, so too were my fellow classmates, as a rumor spread that our pamphlet had been circulated by the secret service to prevent the demonstrations. Between 500 and 600 students began to march from Kabul University towards the downtown of Kabul despite our efforts, towards a place that once upon a time had been home to the voices of dissent without repression, picking up high-school kids along the way. Within a few kilometers they were surrounded by the police. This time the protesters were lucky, as the police left their guns holstered for the most part. But they did turn on the water hoses, and beat the students back with their bully sticks. Some were able to run away, but about two hundred were caught and sent to Policharki prison. In another incident one high-school girl, Naheed, was shot dead.

To show our solidarity and to express our deep rage against the government, we decided to do a special pamphlet. At the same time, our organization was able to identify some active students and the members of other active organizations around the university in an effort to build a steadily more united front. This was not an easy mission: the secret police were looking for us and we had become a higher and higher priority for them over time. And even more than the police spies, the communist students were actively working to find the center of our organization.

After what the government did to those young people, everybody began to agree with our idea of striking without marches. To make sure the demonstrations ended, as they only ever led to death, we worked hard to get everybody in the university on the same page. There were some smaller groups of students who were active at the university too, and we wanted to bring them closer to our main organization. All the while, we were dodging the heavy investigations of the KGB and Afghani secret service, which had picked up after the demonstrations. I was informed that a couple of anti-government groups had agreed to meet with us. A meeting was set with each of them, and it went really well.

Two of the meetings were with groups of just students, like us, only in smaller numbers, and they agreed to become part of our bigger association. The third meeting was with a law student who was living a few miles from our house. Some of our friends had a bad feeling about him. They kind of knew him from high school, where he was an unpopular student for many reasons. I met with him anyway though and it seemed to go well. He too came to an agreement with us, joining our ranks with his friends. A few more times I met with each of the groups to solidify our plan. After the consolidation, our reputation found itself in a very good place and our communication with the student body became much more fluid.

Our pamphlets were being distributed by the thousands. We had been setting weekly meetings among about twenty of us to keep everyone abreast of what was going on. A lot of what I wrote about in the pamphlets came from those meetings. Once they were written, the printer ran off a few thousand copies and brought them back to me. We then all took our share of the documents and gave them out to our connections; then they gave them to their connections, and so forth, to make sure nobody had to distribute a massive number, which would increases the chances of being caught.

The pamphlet following the police beating of the student protestors was truly emotional. Its point of greatest sorrow was over Naheed. The pamphlet was the most public display of grief that young girl would ever receive. It was only recently that the government would even give the body back for the family to bury them – typically they were taken away for a mass burial somewhere. But even now when a body was returned to the family, they did not allow the families to have a public burial. If the family attracted any attention to the funeral, they were arrested themselves.

If anyone shed tears at the funeral, however privately, they risked being killed themselves – such was the fearsome control the government had over the people. Mourning parents, especially a tearful father, were at a very high risk of imprisonment and death. Government agents would be present, watching. If the tears were hidden and came without any level of anger or talk of the murder, then normally nothing would happen. But if there was even the slightest hint of rancor, any word of opposition to the government, then the parent would soon suffer the same fate as their child.

So I turned from activist to poet once again, and filled the pages with something I felt needed to be said against the brutality now becoming an everyday occurrence. I wrote "*Maderm Ber Marge Betaboot Farzandat Mqanal— — Bash Yakdam Rose Tajlil Shaheedan Merasad,*" which means (roughly, without the true sense of poetry) "Mother don't be sad, don't shed tears because you are not allowed to give your child a proper burial, soon it will be time that we can celebrate their martyrdom, their sacrifice."

The protests increased the government repression, but also solidified our resolve. We became far more active in different kinds of anti-government activities. Mom doesn't know exactly what is going on, but she has a feeling that we are actively involved in something. I have my own room now in the back of the building, close to the yard's gate, one built just for me. The privacy in there allowed my friends to come and go as was needed. Mother noticed that, and increasingly began visiting my room to try and figure out exactly what was happening. Every time she asked me I denied having anything to do with the anti-government movement. She begged and pleaded with me to stop whatever it was that I was doing. "They will not have any mercy son," she said, "Look, they have killed tens of thousands of innocent people. Do you think they will mind killing you? Please son, stop it!"

I could hide it no more: I had to tell her, though I knew that my explanation would likely fall upon deaf ears. "I am begging you," she continued, "If they kill you, what would my life become without you?" She added more and more, cutting into my heart, "My life will be over. Please son, I am begging you, please, please, please!" The more she spoke, the more worried she made me. One might claim that if they themselves were in this situation that their resolve would be stubborn, and that they would care not for their own lives, but I believe anyone who truly cares about their community cares also for their own lives. If I was caught, or killed, I thought to myself, what would happen to my Mom, and my brothers, and my sisters. I played a special and important role in my house. But I also had a responsibility to all those that did not have the access that I did, and did not have the luxury of waiting out the Soviets, ducking my head when the bullets flied.

I was a part of this country, a part of these people. I could not just sit and worry about my own life – and who could say that I would not simply die from a stray bullet the next time the crowds formed near my home or school? "Mom," I said to her, "do you know what is going on in our country? A foreign invasion has taken over. Tens of thousands of our innocent people have been slaughtered so far. Nobody is safe." Yet, with my mother, it doesn't make any difference what I say. She was a mother; she just wanted to save her son. She insisted that I should not do anything against the government, no matter what.

I could only reply, "Mother let me ask you a question. If a burglar broke into our house and then, while he was stealing our stuff, he started beating on you; you are putting up resistance and he pulls you by your hair and beats on you, what would I do? Should I say 'oh, he has a gun, so I should be quiet and let him do whatever he wants to do with my Mom?' No, Mom, I will jump! I would rather die before you. I feel that way for you, and my country too. I owe my life to both of you. That is exactly what is going on and this is the only thing I will not listen to you on Mom. I love you, I do whatever you tell me to do, but not this time. You do not have the right to forbid me from standing up for my country. Our country is our mother, your mother and my mother." After that day, mother stopped telling me to quit. Instead, she turned her attentions to praying for my safe return.

Poor Mom, she did not know that I was not alone. Her whole family, except for her youngest son, was active against the occupation that the Evil Empire had brought onto our soil. My two younger brothers are very active in their high-school, my younger sister in her high-school, and my older brother at the university. Thank god she did not know about that, I don't think she ever would have slept again if she did.

Then, one day at about noon, I was waiting for Muhinauldeen and the pamphlets to be brought to me. It was about half an hour before my friends would swing by to pick up their shares and begin the distribution. It didn't always happen at my house, but as we were looking to gain as little attention as possible, this day in particular we were running it out of my new little room.

I heard a noise at the door and assumed it was my friend coming to help with the task, when suddenly the door burst open. As if the military planes had flown so low they had blasted beneath my roof, a dozen secret service agents rushed at me with machineguns drawn. Five or six more leap over our fence and up on the roof of the house. For some reason, I was not surprised—I knew why they were here. The entire family just watched, none of them in shock, as they quickly handcuffed me and warned everybody else not to move. Only my youngest brother, in the second grade at the time, was confused.

The agents then carefully entered the rest of the rooms to check for anything of interest. For an hour they search the entire place, as I quietly stand and watch. Three things worry me. My youngest brother is so scared and worried. I quietly look into his eyes, but don't know how to comfort him. Second, my heart is breaking for my Mom. Her son was now at university and could soon become a doctor, meaning she could relax a little, and I was taking that son away from her. But she was not showing an inch of retreat in her face, even if I knew her heart had sunk. She was only pressing her hands hard against each other, the same thing she did whenever she felt helpless. I remember one time when my younger brother hit a tree as he was running and just fainted, as my Mom shouted for help she pressed her hands in the same way.

The third thing I am worried about is that at any moment Muhinauldeen might open our door and come inside with thousands of pamphlets, or that any of my other friends would come to pick them up. That would be disastrous. But there were armed men on the roof, who could be seen from far away, with the purpose of keeping people away – little did they know that the people they would keep away would help our cause, not theirs.

They rushed to me as if they already knew my face. Mother's face slowly turned white as a ghost, as if she had lost her spirit and her life, even if there was no retreat in her eyes. As she presses her hands over and over again, my younger sister cries and curses them, no matter how I try to silently calm her down. I do not want someone to curse back at her or beat her. She does stop in time. As she does I see that the little face of my youngest brother is red; he is scared and just watching. The two of us were very close.

And all the while the agents were searching our house; I simply prayed to God that nobody else showed up at my door. A second breath of relief came when I saw that the military jeeps were parked in an obvious fashion out in front of the house—certainly they would not be oblivious to that, even if they missed the guards on our rooftop.

After an hour's search they could find nothing, as I was not in the habit of keeping anything around my family. The only thing I could see them pick out from one of our bedrooms was a notebook with a red cover: I don't know what it is, and am a little worried. I told my siblings that they should never keep anything related to our associations in the home but more than anything I am worried about the one thing that did happen to be in the house that day: a couple of pages paper that had the material of our new pamphlet, the same pamphlets I was expecting Muhinauldeen to deliver today.

Those were in our metal fire place. I put them there because Mom needed paper to light the fire. I was so worried about someone finding it as proof that I was the writer of the pamphlets. Though the stack had not arrived yet, we had not been able to burn the evidence that they were even on their way. I cursed myself, knowing they were there. I prayed they did not go to the fireplace… but at the very last moment, someone did just that. They had my papers in hand. At least, I thought, my writing was usually crowded and barely legible. Paper was so scarce in Kabul, and we were so poor, that I was writing and rewriting on the top of those words again and again until I finalized it. The only part totally readable was that poem of mine about Naheed.

After the search they took me with them. My mother was visibly shocked, as my youngest brother sat petrified and my younger sister cried out at them, "One day you guys will pay for your crimes, you traitors!" No matter how I tried, I could not get her to stop this time. I was able to whisper to my younger brother Rahmath to go and tell the others so that they didn't show up at our home before they took me away. They needed to be on high alert.

I was escorted by around a dozen armed guards inside a Russian-built military jeep away from the house. As soon as the jeep left, the head of the team leaned over me and said, "When we were being captured by the Khalqis (Amin's faction that had persecuted the current party in power before his removal) our sisters were not allowed to cry. Then, during the interrogations, they hung weights on our balls."

Automatically I knew he was a Parchami, and that he was complaining about the Khalqis. I figured quickly that it was a good thing that he had been put in jail a few months back, as he would know the pain and be somewhat more sympathetic. But as I tried to reply, I received a strong punch to the right side of my face. "There is no Khalqi or Parchami, there is only *Hezbi Democratic-e-Khalqi Afghanistan.*" Then, there was a long silence. I did not say another word. I knew that this second guy was a Khalqi, and by talking to and through me they were able to extend the old argument that had been entrenched for so long. Parchamis were now in charge, but being pressured by the KGB not to stir up sectarian divisiveness.

We were heading toward downtown as I sat quietly thinking. I knew I had a tough interrogation ahead of me. I had heard from others that they could beat people to death. To be honest, I was terrified, but far more worried about my Mom. And then, in the middle of it all, I began to try to figure out who was spying on us – who told the communists who we were? It was as if the entire organization was infected now. I needed some way of getting word back to my friends. Since the secret service stormed our house close to the time when I was supposed to receive thousands of pamphlets, they likely knew it was going to happen.

There were a limited number of people who knew about this. First, there were the twenty close friends who led the associations with me. But we had been together from the first days, so it could not be one of them. The only other people that possibly knew were three other students, the ones representing the smaller circles of students. They had also agreed to spread the pamphlet. They didn't know that the pamphlets came to my house though, but they could have guessed it, because I told them that around two o'clock I would send them their share. Two of them were going to get it from another member of our association, but one, Taher Gotak, would get it directly from me. I was supposed to see him somewhere a couple miles away between one and two o'clock.

After a couple miles, the Jeep turned to make a quick stop in front of a building. This was right where I was supposed to meet Taher (the same guy my friends did not have a good feeling about) for the distribution of the materials. That one stop told me that either Taher or someone close to him was the spy. During the short stop one of the agents went to the back of the building for only a few moments before coming back, and we departed again. We passed downtown Kabul, and in another twenty minutes the Jeeps stopped in front of a modern looking, nice building I had never seen before.

I read the sign: "Khade Shash Darak." This was one of the branches belonging to the central secret service, called "Khad" at that time. They escorted me inside, then to the basement. They opened a door and told me to get into a cell. They locked the door behind me. The sound was deafening, and shocked me back out of my mind into the world around me.

There were four other people in the room, who quickly greeted me with a "*Salaamalekum*," and I answer back. One of the men is an older guy with a long beard, another one is younger, tall, and has a turban and with a long beard; the other two are very young kids. I hesitated for a moment, but eventually just sat down on the ground. Everybody was quiet.

About an hour later the door opened and this tall, big guy got inside. I saw the papers that were picked from the fireplace in his hands. "Where are the papers?" he asked me.

"You have them in your hands," I answered.

With a quick move he began kicking me as hard as he could as I covered up as best I could, "Not this, you are not here only for this! I am talking about the thousands of pamphlets!"

I tried to play dumb, as if I did not know what he was talking about, but the cursing and beating continued. My body was in shock, but the pain eventually got worse. The kicks and the slaps were merciless. As I was against the wall of the cell, the thought went through my head that "I am about to die". And then, just as suddenly as he entered, the man left without a word, locking the door.

As my mind ran round in circles, coming up with plan after plan after plan, the light started to fade in my cell. Pros and cons, what to say and what not to say—every permutation of my situation was playing out inside my mind. I'd always thought of myself as more than one person – never just one. From the time I was a child I would go inside my head and debate the situations that had befallen me, during times of stress especially. When mother and father would fight, I had my place of safety right there inside of me. It extended itself to times of peace, reading my beloved poetry books, asking questions of myself and thinking hard about the answers. And those people inside of me, grilling each other and laughing at the results, could never allow me to be lonely.

They stood by me through a lot of things in life, and this time they helped me plot. They helped me strategize.

The cell was terrible. It was small and cramped, damp and unclean. It was the first time I had ever been behind a locked door that I couldn't open. Although someone in my mind reminded me of the days that my brother and I would trap the migratory singing birds each spring. The little birds would just thrust themselves, over and over again, into the cage, trying to fly. Never once did they succeed.

Eventually a sudden voice began to argue with someone in the hall. The voice was furious without violence, as if their anger had been left impotent by intimidation and exhaustion. Someone in return argued "Why did you people betray us, why did you let the Russians into our country?" For the first time since the arrest my heart dropped from my chest... as I recognized the voice. It was my brother, Rahmath. The individuals inside my head began the quiver – how stupid is he? How can he think this will help? How can he come to the lair of these damn killers!

They knew about the pamphlets, and now I knew they were patiently taking in my brother's rant and listening for how much he really knew, as well as how he felt about the Russians and the communist regime, so they could make guesses about my own thinking and involvement, as well as the role of my family in it all. We did what we could: to play a hero in here would be suicide. Who would hear our voices, when even our bodies might never escape this place? The heroic thing now was to do everything possible to save the people you know and stay alive – as a gladiator and the tiger in the middle of the ring, one must cheat death in order to truly speak again. The resistance must only go so far as not cooperating, I said to myself; and not begging for mercy, as one must remember that they are representing the pride of a nation, but no further than that. Without hesitation I knocked the door as hard as I could. The guard opened the door in rush to see what was going on. I just see my brother in the hall arguing with the same guy who did beat me few hours ago. . His glance immediately turned to mine – without a word, my brother stopped talking. He raised his head a little and his jaw tightened. Finally he understands, frozen in place

"I need to use the washroom," I said. The guard escorted me out to do so.

I barely slept that night. Instead of engaging with the different parts of me inside my head, I instead thought of my mother, my family, my friends. Nobody came to me during those hours, and I was able to think more clearly without the beatings. Brick by brick I built my strategy, calculating what responses would work best, and examining them to see if the mortar of logic would connect them with enough strength. I was never one to tell a lie, but there was no choice anymore. There had to be lies… excellent, excellent lies.

In the middle of the next morning, another person opened the door, and read my name. Once I answered him, he asked me to follow him to a jeep outside. My younger brother Rahmath was already there inside the car. We greeted each other with a low tone, as if we didn't know each other. The jeep began to move and I whispered with him to find out why he too was caught. "They came back a couple hours after they took you and picked me up." I asked him what they had on him. He responded that, "There was a notebook with a list of the students who were working with us in Habibia high-school."

This made me furious—I had made it explicit as possible that no one should ever keep such a list, and for my brother himself to do it? But it was too late for harsh words, and the situation was tense as it was. "Rahmath" I whispered, "Don't tell them that the notebook is yours. I will answer. You don't know anything. Just zip it." My goal was to control the interrogation as much as I could. Because if he said one thing and I another, it would give the upper-hand to the interrogator. There was a second reason too—I wanted to ensure that my brother did not have a major case. I did not want them to have reasons to torture my brother and possibly, now have a reason not to let my brother go. With two sons gone, my mother would die of heartache. I whispered again, asking him if my older brother was caught too. He answered that he was alerted by family members and had gone into hiding. That brought me a sliver of peace, especially as I knew that he would not be yet another complication for my plans.

In a few more minutes we were in front of the main Khad, Khad-e-Sedarat—the mother brain for the Afghani secret service which was run directly by KGB. I knew this place. It was located in the heart of Kabul. This was the place where many of those thousands of innocent Afghans were taken by the communists in order to be sent to Policharki Jail or simply to the backwaters to be shot. The building stood like an owl perched about a field of mice, haunting Afghans and providing them with a reminder that nothing had been safe for many, many years now. I remembered, when I was a free man, that each time I passed this area, I tried to imagine the interrogations and pray for those inside being tortured. My prayers asked God to make things easier on them, and perhaps even save their lives. But today my mind would have to focus on this for far longer, as I was to encounter the sheer and brutal reality of what truly lied beyond these feared gates.

The gates opened for the jeep, and after another hundred feet there was a second to pass through. The guards next opened the jeep doors for us to get out. My brother and I were separated, led across the huge area filled with buildings. The guard took my brother into one of them, as I was taken into another. Another half acre or so forward were even more buildings. There was no bustling activity in here – no beehive of energy, sinister or otherwise. There was only empty, stern authority. One building had a few rooms at one side, another was two stories tall and about 90 feet in length. In front of it was a Russian tank and several very young armed soldiers. They were also Russian. The rooms along the side of the building I was escorted by had room after room, each about ten feet wide, one after another after another. You could feel the ghosts inside. At the very last cell the guard opened the door, requesting I enter.

The door locked behind me, once again, and I feel more present than I had ever felt before in my life. There is a light switch but I don't turn it on. I remained there alone for half an hour until someone else enters – always somebody else, each time, it seemed. There is a desk in there, and the man quickly moves to sit behind it, turning on the light. The man is not that large, about 5'6" with a medium build. He has dark skin, short hair, and a light blue shirt with gray pants. He asks me to sit at the chair on my side of the desk. Of course I oblige him, as he quietly starts writing something on a pad of paper. Once done, he pushes it to me and gives me another pen.

I read the paper: "Who is providing the pamphlets for you?"

I answer: "I don't know."

As I am writing this, he watches so that he already knows what I've written before I push it to him, and as I complete it, I feel a pain in the side of my face. Harder than you can imagine, he has caught me by total surprise, hitting me as I had never been hit before. Then, as if nothing had happened, he took the paper back from me and began to write again.

In the same way, he pushes it back to me: "Which political organization are you working with?" it reads.

As I answer with the pen, he again leers over the top of it to read it as I put it down. I hesitate for a moment... then write "I am not..." Even before I get past the start of the sentence, he lunges again. Even with my hands moving quickly to cover my face, his punch is so powerful that my own hands hit my face as hard as his hand would have.

Then, once again, as if nothing had happened, he began writing something more, but this time he said out loud that he wanted me to sit and read it more carefully: "Who are your superiors?"

I don't know what to do. I know that if he sees me writing the truth, that I have no superiors, he will beat me again. I am looking at the paper a little more deeply, and take more time, as if I was trying to remember the names of the men he wanted to know. "Which superi...." I was not even half way through the second word as he leapt at me again, beating me more continuously. My defense was much better now that I knew what to expect, which seemed to trigger a whole other level of rage. He crossed over to my side of the desk for better reach: kicking me, punching me, slapping me, as if he wanted me to know that he could kill me at any moment, and in as much suffering as he wished.

His frame now appears to be far more imposing. He was taller than I was, and I knew that if I struck back it would only extend the beating. He beat me good for several minutes, and then, as if nothing had happened, he sat back down and started writing again. I want to clean the blood from my nose but there is nothing to clean it with but my hand. The blood is flowing so thoroughly that there is not enough material to my upper shirt to get the blood off my hands. I had to take up the bottom part my long shirt, and began to clean the inside my nose compulsively. Whatever I can think of to waste more time and delay his boxing match, I do.

Pushing the paper over to me again, and with a look of his eyes, tells me to sit. I pick the chair up from the floor, put it back in its place, and sit. It is the first question again: "Who is providing the pamphlets for you?" I read it even more slowly, taking time, as if I was considering the question with care.

"Which pamphlets?"

And without missing a beat, he began to beat me again. With a couple punches and kicks, he knocks me to the floor. Once on the ground, his boot is meeting my flesh indiscriminately as I enter the fetal position, keeping my thighs tightly together to protect myself in between my legs. His kicks send me tumbling across the room, until he bends down to his fists. For a good five minutes, he did nothing but strike me again and again. First I would feel the pain of him striking a new portion of me, and then I would feel the far deeper pain of him striking those same spots again and again. All the protection from pain that shock could give me had disappeared. When he stops, I remained in the same position, still covering my face and hiding my balls in between the thighs.

The room entered another mode of silence, with no other sound but his deep breathing. His breaths are loud: he had thoroughly tired himself in beating me. The breaths remind me of the military planes that flew over Kabul day after day. The next sound I hear is him lighting a cigarette, and starting to smoke. I then hear him putting the papers in a file and leave. Even after the door is locked between the two of us, I waited in that same position. It takes a while before I decide to move, and start examining my damaged body. Everything hurts. I don't know if my ribs are broken, I don't know if anything or everything is broken – I cannot tell through the pain. I did not want to sit. I just kept laying there and thinking about his questions. I just couldn't tell if I was doing the right thing or not.

Still on the floor after several hours, the door opens again. I cannot keep myself from shivering in fear of another round. "Wake up, and have your food," says a new guard, standing there with a plate of food in one hand and a plastic glass of water in the other. I try to sit but it is just so hard to move my body. It hurt even to move a few inches. The guard helps me up as I held onto the leg of the desk and sit myself up against the wall. For a brief moment I thought of refusing to eat, but my hunger made the food look too good to pass up. It is a good size plate of palaw, with a wonderful aroma. In it were big chunks of meat. "If they love me so much, why are they beating me?" I joked with myself. A smile crawls onto my face, but boy, did that smile ever hurt.

As I start to chew, my jaw aches. But the food tastes as good as it looks, and slowly but surely I was going to eat it. There was nothing to clean the grease from my hands, and the blood, spit, and mucus from my nose had dried into a hard crust all over my face; around my lips. In some kind of effort to return to a kind of normality, I rub the grease from my food on my face to soften it up, so that maybe I could clean myself.

My thoughts turned inward and upward to God. "I think I am holding up pretty well," I say to myself. I thank myself for not giving in. "Thanks god, it is not as bad as people were saying it was in here, oh well, people always exaggerate," I said to myself as my smile continued.

As I finish my meal I begin to crave a cup of tea. I had not had one since the arrest, and I was just dying for a cup of it. Those cherished, ideal thoughts soon found themselves stomped into the ground though, as the interrogator returned, this time accompanied by two more men. Not a single word is exchanged, they simply start to beat me—I felt as if the food I had just eaten was stolen from their own kitchen table. Cramped and atrophied, I cannot even pull in to defend myself from their vicious attacks. Instead of remaining in one corner of the cell, I found myself thrust about – up against the walls, over the desk, into the chair… everywhere. A typhoon had picked me up and there was just no way down.

After a long evisceration, one of them tells me to get up and sit in the chair. He is a tall, skinny guy with a very pointy nose. Perched on his nose was a pair of reading glasses. The others quietly watch him with an air of reverence as he talks.

I am not able to sit. I am not even able to turn to my side. My vision is blackening, but still he instructs me to sit. I try, and do, for I am quite afraid that he will make it even more difficult for me. He castigates me: "Up! Don't act like a coward: up like a man!" This, now this... turned my thoughts entirely to anger: I knew that he himself would never stand, and even more so, would never keep another person from extracting his thoughts as if they were figs from a tree.

I slowly turned to my right side, then bent myself over my stomach, and with help of my hands, I went to oblige him. But still, I am not able to. Shouting, he again castigates me, instructing me to sit. Next he himself pulls me up, and I cry out loud from the pain. I am hoping, I am praying, that they don't beat me again. At least not before morning.

The man in charge opened a file and began to read from one of the papers inside: "*Motherm Ber Marg Betaboot Farzandat Manall. Bash Yakdam Rose e Tajlil Shahedan Merasad.*" This was my poem. The one they found in our fireplace, which I had given to my mother to help her start the fire. "Is this yours?"

I play dumb again. I knew they found it at our house, but it was not proof that it was mine. "No, it's not," I replied.

As he comes over to my side of the desk, I do not even raise my hands to cover my face this time. I know he will have his hands round my neck, and there is nothing I can do about it. But instead, he holds me by my two ears and lifts me up. He turns me towards him, looks me directly in the eyes, and asks me again if the poem was mine. I refuse to answer. Keeping his hands on my ears, he begins to kick me hard underneath the knees. He was kicking me right in places that hurt more than anything else before. I quickly realize that this man was a specialist; that he knew how to hurt people. He keeps on with it. I'm not quiet anymore. I cannot take it. Soon, my shouts turn to pleading, and I beg him to let me go. As if he is deaf, he kicks me again and again. The pain is bone deep.

It travels a thousand miles into my legs and, as if the pain were a laser bouncing off a mirror deep within my flesh, scattered and transferred into my whole body. Never were there questions at the same time as the beating. Never. So when he went to ask me once again, the beating stopped – if only momentarily. "Tell me if that is yours! Tell me, tell me!"

I am half dead. I am not even able to say yes, or no. He holds me tight on the ears and hits the back of my heads against the wall. The wall was not concrete, but it was hard, it was bricks. Each time my head hits the wall, I feel as if my brain is going to fly out through my bloody nose. It occurs to me in a flash of pain, that the difference between them beating me for information and beating me to death is not something that I could distinguish here. Any time they raised their hands to me, I could die. After several crushing blows to the head, my memory fades, and I lose consciousness.

In the blackout, I dreamt that I was being arrested again. I saw them taking me away, and my mother crying and shouting and begging them to let me go. They pull me away, but my mother is not letting them go. She is hanging tight to one of them and keeps begging. One of them beings to push her, and she falls to the ground. One guard lifts up with his gun, and another breaks open my head with the blunt end of another.

Suddenly I woke up, my head was pounding. For a moment I could not tell the difference between what was real and what had simply been a dream. There were goose eggs in my scalp, and my jaw continued to ache. My back, my chest, my hands, my arms, my legs, and every other little part of my body was on fire. As I opened my eyes it was totally dark. The pain was made far worse by the shivering of my skin in the cold summer night, there on the icy concrete in only a robe.

Facing out the door, up above there are millions of twinkling stars, shining bright. In Kabul there were not many lights at night, and the stars were far more brilliant. I checked my face again, and the crusted blood now covered thick bruises. My legs were hurting like hell especially. I felt sorry for myself and for the first time, tears were entering the corners of my eyes. But these were unlike any tears I had ever had before – they were hot, they burned my face. I began to think about my family in a different way—I began missing them.

My mother, I missed her with all of my heart, as if I were still a little child waiting for her to come home from work. I missed my younger brother and younger sister especially. My mother though, I missed her so deeply. I remembered on that floor the times when as a little kid I would take with fever, and she brought a cold towel to rub over my face and neck and back. In the morning she cleaned my eyes with a piece of cotton soaked in warm black tea. She combed my hair with her beautiful fingers and held me tight. I was a sick little boy again, alone on the cement floor. I wanted so badly for her to bring me a towel, a warm one to bury my face, my back, my neck, my hands, my arms... I wanted her to clean my face, I wanted her to comb my hair with her beautiful fingers. Yes, I wanted her to take a towel, soak it in warm water, and clean my face — around my mouth, around my eyes. I wanted her to massage my forehead; I wanted her to massage my head with her beautiful fingers, like when I was young and sick. I wanted for her to comb her fingers through my hair.

I looked at the sky again. I look at the sky and the stars. I remembered that when we were young my mother told us that there was a star for every person in the world, a star just for them. Rich or poor, young or old, man, woman, pretty or ugly, there was a star for you in the sky. I remembered that in the summer, my siblings and I would sleep outside underneath the sky. The group of us would just stare up into the darkness, making jokes about each other's stars. We would choose the shiniest ones for ourselves and the smaller ones for others, teasing each other until we fell asleep.

Mother insisted there was a star for every one of us here on earth, and that each one represented God's love. I would tell my older brother that the dimmest one was his, and the brightest one was mine. He would of course find an even brighter one to claim as his own, and an even dimmer star for me. Back and forth we would trade stars the way I think a lot of kids in America trade baseball cards. We would try and scoop each other on the better parts of the sky, and it would often become quite competitive.

On this night far into the future though, I tried to find mine once again, there on the concrete floor, to see how it was doing. It occurred to me that perhaps it wasn't true that everybody had a place up there, though perhaps it was, and in those thoughts I fell asleep.

"Wake up, wake up!" yelled the guard. "Wake up and have your breakfast." I opened my eyes, but I still could not turn my body over. The guard there was a very nice man, and as before, he helped me out, pulling up my broken body so that I could sit.

"I need to go to the bathroom," I said. With a touch of kindness, amplified by the cruelty of the others, he got under my shoulder so that I could slowly stand. With his help, I started walking toward the bathroom.

When I came back it was as if God had answered a prayer: there awaiting me was a cup of tea, and piece of bread. I held the wall, sat on the ground, and then leaned back against the wall. The guard handed the precious cup to me as well as the bread. The tea was hot, and I sip it carefully. The bread is tough, and my jaw is so swollen that I simply cannot eat. I handed it back to the guard, as there was no point in me having it in my hand.

Around 8:30 or 9:00 the door opened. Standing there was my interrogator, as if he had just gotten to work and was prepared to get right to it. Without saying anything, he sat down in his chair and opened the file he always had in his hand. As if I was just some menial task he'd done once weeks ago, he set about refreshing his memory as to where to begin. "Sit in your chair," he said finally, without looking at me.

I bent myself with difficulty, and used the desk to help me sit. Again, just like the day before, he started writing on a piece of paper, and pushed it to me. I read what he wrote, and it was the same question he asked me first the day before. I read, and read, and read, taking as much time as possible. I was barely able to move the pen on the paper. But I forced myself, and answered the same as I had the day before. I was ready to toss my hands up towards my face, but this time, he did not beat me.

He then wrote down another question, and when I wrote the answer and raised my hands, again he did not beat me. He asked me all kinds of questions, but about nothing new, and I continued to answer the same way. I memorized each answer I wrote down, but in the middle of it, the interrogator began to speak instead.

"Whose notebook is this?" he asked, holding up the book my brother had told me about.

The notebook has a red cover; it was the one I saw them flipping through during the search of our home. "I do not know," I responded.

"Who are the names in this book," he replied.

"What names?" I asked. The man held open the book and showed me. On the top of the page, in very beautiful hand writing, read "List of the Members of Habibia High-School Associations." I looked at the long list of names that went on for several pages — it was amazing how many people we had been able to bring into the fold. But something instantly strikes me – this is not my brother's handwriting. My brother's handwriting was a far cry from this – as sloppy as could be. I never thought I would be so happy about something like this.

The other positive thing was that the list itself was not nearly enough to find someone, because in Afghanistan the majority of us did not have last names. We only identified people with their father's name, or their grandfather's name if they had the same father names. So if there was a Muhammad Amin on the list it didn't much matter because, at that high-school there were dozens of Muhammad Amins. You needed to know more than just their name to distinguish this particular Muhammad Amin from the others. Unless we told them exactly which Muhammad Amin we had on the list, they would not be able to identify them. So I felt comfortable, because they can not just go to that high school and simply arrest all these kids.

Every question put to me about the notebooks received the same responses that I gave to the questions yesterday. Finally he asked me, "Who do you think this notebook belongs to?" Knowing my older brother was safely away, and wanting to take the heat off my younger one and myself, I finally give them a little bit more.

I answered, "I don't know, perhaps my older brother. I have seen a notebook like this with him." I did not want them to create a task-force or anything, so told them I really didn't know for sure. No matter how far he went, I knew the communists might be able to find him. Writing it down, I was able to push it back to him without fear of having another stiff pain in the side of my face. He asked a lot of questions, then left. It had been about two hours since he had first arrived. As soon as he is gone, I spent every moment possible just repeating my answers over and over again, ensuring I could remember them for next time. And I knew there would be a next time. Where possible, I tried to come up with even better ones than before, answers that would make it appear as if I was giving in a little bit more.

The door opened again a short while later, and a soldier entered the room with some food. The meal was just as good as the day before: palaw, with a little sabzi, which is excellently cooked spinach, and a glass of water. Again the chewing is nearly unbearable, but I get through it. Unlike the bread, this food was truly worth it. After the food, my eyes shuts, and I feel myself returning to sleep.

The opening of the door awakens me. It is my interrogator, once again. I pull myself up, lean against the wall, and then I sit in the chair without being told. Without paying any attention to me, he just starts writing again. He writes me the same questions, and I am writing the same answers. He keeps repeating the questions and I repeat the same answers. Once again, he does not beat me. Around 4pm, he closes his file and leaves. Again I get a chance to lie on the floor and close my eyes. The pattern from before began to repeat itself, as I put my entire being into remembering my answers and crafting the best possible responses. I thought that if they found no contradictions, they might think I was telling the truth. Otherwise, they would likely be able to draw out the truth from within the variations of my answers without me even knowing it.

I pass out once again, and wake to poisonous thoughts about the interrogations. Rubbing my shoulder, I tried to encourage myself. I wanted to convince myself that the worst was over. That I would soon heal and that everything would be okay.

Around eight o'clock, the guard brought me dinner again: a shourba, which is a meat soup, and a full nan bread. The food just got better and better – this was far better than what almost every other Afghan could afford to eat at home. I cut the bread into bit-sized pieces and soak it in the soup. This made it far easier for me to eat.

It is around ten o'clock, the door opened again and three people walked in. As they turned on the lights I could see them more clearly: once again it was the man with the reading glasses and his cohorts.

This, I knew, was not a good sign. I pulled myself up and leaned against the wall. "Up and sit in the chair," the man with the glasses commanded me. With difficulty, this time I was able to. The man with the glasses pulled something new out of my file – a copy of our pamphlet. "Do you know this *Shabnama?*"

It was the new issue. My heart shuddered, I panicked, and I began furiously thinking about how they would have gotten a printed copy of it. Either Muhinauldeen had been caught or, something that would be more preferable news, our association had spread the *Shabnama* and the secret service got a copy. Neither is very good at all for me, as they have seen something from my home in rough draft make it into the printed format. With sarcasm, he read the poem aloud once more, this time from the printed page.

"*Maderam ber marg be taboot farzandat manal Bash yakdam roze tajleel shahidan merasad!* So do you think that we will lose power? Do you think that you little people will topple us, and your mother will come to your grave and celebrate your martyrdom?! Do you really think that?" As he continued, the man got closer and closer to me. I could see a deep anger in his eyes. I had nothing to say, remaining perfectly silent. I knew that anything I said would only increase his levels of rage.

Once again he held me by my ears. He held tight as he did the day before, This time however, he only slapped me. Over and over he slapped me, as he taunted me with the poem out loud. "*Maderam ber marge betaboot farzandat Mana... Bash yakdam rose Tajlil shahedan merasad.*" He read that stupid poem again and again, bruising my face. "Do you, do you really think that your Mom will celebrate your martyrdom? Do you?" he said.

I remember now that when we were in elementary school, our teachers were always beating us. The majority of them did it, but the Quran and the Pashto teachers were the worst. When they beat us, they hurt us a lot. But we, the boys, had to hold ourselves together. We wanted to make sure not to shout and cry, and never to ask for mercy. If you cried then the classmates would tease you, calling you a little girl. We needed to be tough.

Usually male teachers were the ones who beat us, but in the sixth grade we had a female teacher, Amina Jan, who was worse than all of them. One day I got into a fight with one of my classmates. During the next hour, we had her for geography. When she got in, she noticed that Hafiz, my classmate, was crying. She asked him why, and he pointed at me, "He beat me with a rock on my head." After examining his head and finding a large lump, you could see the rage building. She sent another one of the students to fetch some *choob* - little tree branches, half an inch thick and two to three feet long.

Our principal's office always had plentiful of that. The guy brought back like four of them. She then asked me to come to the front of the room and hold my palms up. Down came the switch as powerfully as she could swing it onto my right hand, and then my left hand, and then my right, and then my left. When one branch broke, she picked up another one, and then another one, and then another one. My hands screeched in pain, but my mind was far harder to etch with her fierce nature than my little hands. I just held each palm up without hesitation until every switch had broken.

She then struck my face with the broken piece and said, "*Broo goom sho*" – get lost. As I was sat back down the guy who was sitting next to me whispered: "She hit you seventy two times!" He was proud of me. Nobody wanted to have a coward for a friend. That day in front of the interrogator, I had the same resolve. I just repeated that number over and over again in my mind: *seventy-two times*. It did not take a man to stand; it took a man to never ask for mercy. Again and again he slapped me, but I would not begrudge him a shout or a yell as I had the night before that. Soon he was kicking my knees again, reading my poetry again and again "*Maderam ber marg betaboot farzandat manal...*"

More than anything I hated it when he read that damn poetry. I was beginning to hate myself for being a poet in the first place. I regretted writing that stupid little thing so much. The man laid into me as if I were a training bag. Inside my head there was another battle going on, between the part of me that would not budge and the other trying to bring new words to my lips like "*Akh, Akh* please stop, you are killing me." Eventually the stronger part of me gives in. The front of the classroom was nothing compared to this. I began to cry and shout. I could not stand on my legs anymore and my ears were carrying my entire bodyweight now. But he would not let go, and simply began to strike my head against the wall again. Snot began to fly out of my nose every time he thrust it back against the wall. Again he kept repeating that fucking poetry.

Then, he stopped, and while still holding me by my ears, returned to his own little spell "do you think that we will lose, do you think that you guys are going to topple us… no, no we will stay. We will not lose, because the Red Army of the Soviet Union is behind us!"

From every part of my being I wanted to shout aloud and say "you will lose motherfucker, you will, if I am alive or dead it does not matter, if my Mom can celebrate me or not, it does not matter, but yes you will lose!" Does not matter who is behind you, the Red Army or the White Army, you will lose mother fucker. But I do not. It was tough enough on me already; I did not want to make it harder. At some point afterwards, as he repeatedly beat my head against the wall, I lost consciousness again.

When I woke the room was dark once again. Once again, I was cold and shivering. My hands were between my legs trying to stay warm, but there was moisture there now. At first I thought it was sweat, but taking my hand up to my nose I realized it was urine. With all my might I try to flip myself towards the door so that I could see the sky, but it is nearly impossible. Anything I do now carries extraordinary pain. Finally I was able to get myself onto my other side. As I looked outwards, again I saw the sky was full of stars. But I was no longer trying to find my star. I no longer cared about the stars or if anybody had a star in the sky or not. This time I was looking into the stars to find God, the creator of these stars, and to see if he was watching all of this or not. I wanted God to look me in the eye.

I yelled at him inside my head: "God, how can you patiently just watch all of this? How can you let all of this to happen? How can you take all of this? How you can quietly sit and watch them do this!" Tears were once again burning the bruises and abrasions all over my face. That night it even began to burns the corner of my eyes. I had given up on life. After berating my God, I simply asked him to take my life away from me. It was my only wish. I wanted nothing more, "Is that too much? Can you please? I thought taking life was the easiest thing for you. Please God, take me. This is the only wish I have, just take me. Is it too hard for you? Please… take me." I never thought that one day I would beg God to take my life. I never thought that one day it would be my best wish, my only wish.

I thought I was so brave, that I could represent the Afghan people. Now with wet pants, not remembering if it happened during the interrogation or afterwards when they left me there to die, I had no idea how I was supposed to do that. What if my friends found out that I simply could not hold myself during the interrogation; found out I peed myself? What if my mother found out that her brave son simply peed? I wondered if she would forgive me, or ever be proud of me.

I didn't want to see anything anymore. I just shut my eyes with the hope that they never opened again.

The following morning I am not dead. God was not that generous to me. The guard shouted that it was breakfast time again. I did not want to wake up that morning. I wanted to curse the guard, the interrogator, and all the other cowards that would not stand up to a fair fight—that hid behind the skirt of the invaders that like little children. For a moment I act as if I were dead so that I did not have to answer him. He shook me carefully on the shoulder. "Wake up, it is breakfast time, wake up."

I continued to play dead.

He shook me harder, "Are you okay?"

I want to shout: "Can't you see me? Can't you tell? Are you blind?"

He shook me a little more, I opened my eyes. My whole face was swollen – my eyes and cheeks were stiff. I could barely see, I could barely talk. He bent down and pulled me up. I guess I have to wake up, I thought. I guess I needed to take my breakfast, I thought. I guess I have to pull myself up and make myself ready for another round, I thought. This time I am going to the ring like a loser, like a coward, only to be beaten, to pee, to cry, to beg for mercy, I thought. I was reduced to nothing.

I needed to have my breakfast so I could stand for him, at least for the first round, so he could enjoy beating me, so he could read that damn poetry of *Maderm bermarg betabot farzandat manal*; so he could hit my head against the wall and tell me they could not lose because they were hiding behind the iron skirt of the Red Army; so that he could tell me that my mother, who I alternatively looked to care for myself, would never have a chance to bury me. That she would never be able to mourn for me.

Yes, I need to wake up, I thought. I forced myself: I wanted God to see my torture once again, quietly and patiently. I forced myself up, and up, and up, and stood on my feet. In repetition of the last morning I spoke: "I need to go to the rest room." The guard kindly tried to hold me under the shoulder to help me go to the bathroom, but with a move of my shoulder, I refused the help. I kept walking, as hard as I could. I wanted to hurt myself, just like that skinny weasel with the glasses. I washed my face. I rinsed my mouth. I spit. It was mixed with blood. I walked back to the room again under my own power, feeling every inch of myself in need of attention in a place where the only attention would make it far worse. Once I returned, the guard left the cup of tea and bread for me on the desk and walked out. I sat on the floor and leaned against the wall. I felt so helpless. I felt so lonely. Tears burned my cheeks. I stopped caring and simply let stream.

After an hour my interrogator showed up. He told me to sit in the chair. I refused. I was not able, but even if I was, I likely still would never have done so that morning. I simply said, "You can just start beating me here today, on the floor. I am not able to stand."

He looked at me, and came to my side of the desk, "What's wrong?"

"Nothing," I replied, "but I am not able to sit."

"Tell me exactly why not?" he replied.

I spit on the floor, all of it is blood. "This is what is wrong with me."

He stood for a while, and then left. I was broken and sad. Then, I looked at a sign on the wall again as if for the first time, "Nobody can torture you during an investigation: if someone does, let us know!"

"Yes, let us know!" I thought. How? Where should I complain? I smiled again, but this time in a more jaded way.

After another half hour a guard brought me some medication, and asked me to take it. He then provided me a glass of water and a blanket before closing the door. I wrapped myself up and just laid dead.

The guard shouted again, "Lunch time!"

Waking, my breakfast is still sitting on the desk, and beside that is my lunch. The hunger burned inside of me, but I did not want to eat. I wanted to die. Inside of me another struggle amongst the many me's: eat, no, eat, no. But it was amazing this power inside of you to live, this love of life inside you. It tackles the need to die with some veracity and always wins. My food was now cold, as it had been sitting there for a couple hours.

I looked around and picked the plate of food. I opened my mouth and placed a little bit inside, chewing a little, and then swallowing. My cold cup of tea was there too, blinking to me like a luscious bikini clad woman. I picked it up and sipped. It was sweet, and brought a sprinkle of joy into that darkest of days. Little by little, I finished everything. The blanket felt so good.

As soon as my food was finished, I laid on the floor. I squeezed myself to a smaller size to save my body heat, with my hands between my legs. I wanted to see if they had tortured me between the legs, but I moved each ball and neither screamed in pain. I only woke again for dinner. A soup, bread, a cup of water. The guard gave me some additional medication, and would not leave until he saw me take it. I let the soup get cold, and then soaked the bread in it. Afterwards, I knocked on the door and told the guard that I needed to go to restroom. With his help this time I go, and when we return, he left me alone. I leaned against the wall for a little, and then went to sleep again. Like no other time in my life, I was able to go to sleep like a dead person. Usually I would wake up at two or three o'clock in the morning. My mind was always like an alarm clock, but in this cell I did not wake up at all. Only the guard woke me that night, and that was for breakfast. I spit again, and the blood was gone. I could stand a little easier too.

I looked up at the sky and was no longer mad at God. I saw that he was generous, and I had simply asked for something I would not want for very long. I smiled a bit, but the pain in my lips stopped me from doing so for very long. The specter of the pain remained.

My whole body is now being pulled back into the story again as I tell it. I have my breakfast, some medication, and then lay back. My daytime interrogator enters, and I realize that I know none of their names. They don't call each other by name, and it occurred to me that if they did, it might give someone they were interrogating recourse – the get their names out there for retaliation. Instead, they simply refer to each other as *Lala*. The term, as I mentioned at the beginning of the book, meant "brother". In Afghanistan in partic-ular, it referred to an older brother that had a lot of power over you – and whom you were supposed to have a deep level of respect for. In your life authority came from, in order, your Dad, then God, then Quran teacher and the Mosque Mullah, then your Pashto teachers, then your Lala.

Sometimes friends called each other Lala out of respect. In those days the word was kind of out of date in Kabul city. At first Afghan communists called each other "friend", just like in the days of Lenin and Stalin when the Russians used the word "comrade". But since then that word had become a hateful joke, since after the killings of tens of thousands of Afghans at the hands of the Afghan communists even these communists seemed too shy to use the word "friend". Instead, they use the word Lala. Ironic, as this word was also a favorite of gamblers, thugs, and illiterate boys who think of them-selves as tough. More importantly, the word was really common among Charci guys, the ones who smoked hashish. Yes, my morning time Lala was here now. When I saw him, I took off my blanket, and sat in the chair. Without saying a word, he sat as well, and opened the file, making himself busy for a few minutes, again as if he was refreshing his memory.

He wrote something and, as usual, he pushed the paper back to me. I read and took some time with it, before writing my answer. As I wrote the answer I prepared myself for his strikes, but no punch came my way. Lala wrote another question, I wrote the answer, and in the same way Lala did not lunge. All the questions were the same as before, and I wrote the exact same answers in response. Everything was memorized, 100%. A couple hours passed before he wrapped his file and left. Lunch came, my palaw, and I ate without hesitation.

A couple hours later my Lala came again: same questions, same answers. A couple of hours passed, he wrapped the file, and left. They kept me for two more days in that same room. The day after that, my afternoon interrogation with Lala ended with him telling the guard to take me to a different building, the name of which I cannot recall anymore. I followed the guard as he walked towards the end of the building. There he opened a small door to an unpaved road and turned right. Before him there was an iron gate about fifteen feet wide.

Two armed guards were standing there. My guard talked with them a moment and then the two opened the gate. As we entered I saw little rooms on three sides of the building. They were each different in size, but all on the same story. I saw that rooms were 12-30 feet wide. There was a little pond in the middle of the small yard around which the rooms were arranged. I see there is a well there with a bucket tied to a rope. The guard walked to the northeast corner of the building, opened a little door, and told me that this would be my room. I saw about ten or twelve people inside, some sitting and some lying. A few of them were asleep.

I say *salaam*, and they greet me in return. All of them were young, very young. Perhaps high-school kids. There are two older men. One is about forty, and I notice immediately that his left arm had been amputated. He introduces himself as Dr. Ahmad Shah Ferhad. I recognize him. I did not know him personally, but I knew his famous Dad. He was a very famous engineer; one of the first Afghan students who were ever sent to Germany to become an engineer. He worked for many years as Mayor of Kabul and he was the one who designed some of our most modern streets inside the city.

The other reason I recognize him is because his Dad was the founder of Afghan Melat, an extremist Pashtun racist political organization (Pashtun organizations that hate all non-Pashtun Afghans). I quickly figure out that Dr. Ahmad Shah was also a Pashtun racist, and to be honest I didn't feel comfortable with racist people. I had learned from my books and my mentors to respect all human beings. The second person that was older than me was Dagerwal Khalil. He was around fifty years old, 5'7", and had an athletic build. He was a military man.

Unlike the interrogation rooms which had concrete floors, this little room was overcrowded with little homemade mattresses, about two by six feet in size, and plenty of mismatched homemade blankets. I sat against a pillow on the wall on one of them. It felt so good. Someone asks my name, I answer. Another one asks the reason why I had been arrested, I said I did not know. I was very cautious about saying anything, as I knew that there might be people there spying for the interrogators. Later on, when I had a chance, one by one I ask some of their names. There are three young men that had been arrested for attending a demonstration. They were all classmates and close friends. One was Fared, a dark and skinny boy, another was named Ali Mohammad, and the other one was, I believe, Sadeq. Sadeq was a singer with a band, something extremely uncommon in Afghanistan. In the whole country we had only a few modern music bands, one being made up entirely of my roommates here at the Khad.

Around eight o'clock in the evening, dinner was served. It was the same shourba. In here they call a couple people from each room to come and then they bring back the food for their roommates. Each room had their turn for the toilets, three times a day. In the morning they let everybody to go out for a couple hours for a walk together, according to my roommates. It felt good to be in the room with other people. After the food, we got a chance to talk a little more. I talked a little with Dr. Ferhad, the Pashtun racist political activist, and I found that he did not sound like a racist at all.

He was more like the people of Kabul. He told me that had lived in Germany for many years and went to university there. His major was, I think, economics. In Germany he completed graduate studies and his wife was a physician, with two young daughters, all still in Germany. We talked a little about his Dad, who was retired and very old now. Deep inside I was a little embarrassed to think that he was a racist, as it now seemed that neither he, nor his Dad, nor anyone in their family shared racist thoughts.

In Afghanistan it was not unusual for people to accept rumors and base their thoughts on those rumors even when faced with the truth. The other older man Dagerwal was playing chess with another one of our roommates. They had this handmade chess set that he eventually taught me to play on, made of the soft inside portion of the bread, and a board hand drawn onto a piece of cardboard. Dagerwal was the only one who could have a chessboard in the room, because he watered all the plants around the perimeter and was knowledgeable about gardening. He was able to get to know a few people in charge of the building and build a good reputation for working hard.

Around ten or eleven o'clock we went to sleep. There were about twelve or thirteen of us all sleeping on six or seven mattress all set up one beside the other. Side by side we lay. My body though, quickly began to itch. Then, as I itched, I saw everybody doing the same. Whether they had not all been there for all that long or I had alerted them to it, somebody finally moved their blanket and began hunting for what it was that was causing the itching. I thought for sure that it was lice, but it was something far worse... We had bed bugs – insects that were four times bigger than lice, like tiny cockroaches, red in color from the human blood they had just gorged on. There were hundreds of them. Every hour or so we would all wake up, move the blankets, and start hunting again. Never did we catch very many of them. As soon as we started hunting them they would quickly run and hide in the cracks of the brick walls...

At eight in the morning, it was again breakfast time. Breakfast was always quick: it only took a few minutes. It was only a cup of sweet tea, a piece of bread, and some hungry prisoners. After the breakfast I was anxious for that walking break I had been told about. I could not wait to go outside and walk with everybody, to see who else was there. More than anything I was trying to see if my brother was there. I wanted confirmation that then had been released, or, a lesser wish, just to see them. At about nine o'clock a guard announced my name and asked me to follow him. He took me back to the interrogation room at the adjacent building. The same room as before.

Again my Lala showed up a little later, and asked me the same questions in the same manner. I answered the same way. Around lunch time he sent me back to the other building. As soon as I was back, I saw that the yard was now crowded. It was still walking time. The guard just let me go and I started walking with the prisoners.

As I was walking, I took a deep look at the crowd, though each set of eyes seemed to be looking curiously back at me. As we passed each other we would say *salaam*. I saw a few of my roommates who I greeted and began to walk with them. I was talking with them but my mind was still somewhere else. Then, I saw my younger brother, with a smile on his lips, coming towards me.

Oh it meant the world to me. I hugged him hard, kept him tight for a moment, kissing him several times. I then gave him a deep look to see if he was alright. No, bruises, no swollen face, no limp... it made me so happy. We just walked together the entire time, until the walking time was over. We talked about everything. I asked him if he was interrogated or tortured. "No," he told me. He was not tortured at all, but he was interrogated a couple of times. From the description of his interrogator, I knew that it was my interrogator: thank God it was not the man with the glasses, but my Lala.

He said he was asked about the notebook and the list of names, but he denied having any information. They also asked him about my older brother's whereabouts, his political views, his friends, and also about me, my political involvements, and my friends. Of course he did not know a thing about me or my brother. He asked me about my interrogations and I told him it was not easy, but it was okay. I didn't want him to be concerned about me: he was just a tenth grader, and it already was hard on him. He whispered to me that one of the boys from his school, who was in his room, was released so he had given our home address to him and asked him to go there and tell our family that we are okay. I shone with pride, as I knew that was exactly what our mother needed to hear.

It was already lunchtime and they told us all to go to our rooms. A couple of people from each room went outside to help bring in our lunch. That famous Khad palaw; that delicious food. When we were walking my brother and I started in on the subject matter and he told me a story. He said that in his room there was an older man who was illiterate and from the rural parts of Kabul. He was a farmer and each day when they were eating the palaw he would tell everybody, "Man, eat it! Eat it, because once you leave this detention you will never find such good food for the rest of your lives!" My brother imitated the man's accent and it made me laugh.

We have our lunch and a couple hours later the guard came back for me, taking me to that same room in the adjacent building. It became my regular schedule for the next six or seven days. Twice a day I was taken for interrogation, but the beatings had stopped. The same questions came at me and the same answers flowed out of me. I was beginning to think they were leaning towards the idea that it was probably my older brother who was in charge of most of the staff. It was not that they thought I was innocent, and I was not expecting them to, but I had finally managed to point them in that direction, and my younger brother had too. That was helping me. They didn't see any reason to kill me or beat me anymore for something I knew very little about.

Life was getting better now. My bruises were almost gone, as was most of my pain, and my recovery didn't seem to have many side effects. What a wonderful creature this human being is. The human being is like rubber: you can pull him and pull him and pull him and it continues to stretch. Before going through all of this, I would never have believed that I was capable to take it all. The test let me know so much about myself, maybe more than anything before it ever had.

In my room I was now very close to everybody there. I was the only one in the building facing interrogations twice daily, and it created some respect for me in the room. My roommates though that perhaps I was someone important. From my bruises they knew I had been beaten badly. They began to trust me with their interrogation stories and sought my advice. Giving advice in there was dangerous for me though, as if my interrogators found me coaching the inmates on how to answer the questions then the days of the vicious beatings were sure to return, but I felt obligated. Most of the kids didn't have a clue, even the older ones didn't know how to answer those tricky questions.

I helped Fared and his musician friends especially as my Lala was their interrogator too. Their case was really easy, but we Afghans are a very simple people. The mind games these well-trained interrogators played on us were more than we could bear in many cases—even though we were so hateful of outsiders, within our communities there was always a common love and trust. To have those that may have picked us up after we scraped our knees when we were younger torturing us and placing us in cramped conditions was something many had never imagined.

They had KGB training and we had just suddenly realized that you couldn't trust your neighbor anymore. They very easily tricked most of us, twisting even simple cases into something the state could hold up as proof of a conspiracy against them. I advised them not to admit that they were part of that demonstration. "Once you admit anything, you are creating a case against yourself. Just say that you guys were onlookers, or that you were just going home and you were picked up anyways." A few days later they were called in for additional interrogations. They were taken in the morning and were brought back late in the afternoon after long days of interrogation.

When they were back, Fared was totally beaten and bruised but the other two were okay. I asked Fared what had happened, but he did not want to talk. He was sad and quiet. Ali Muhammad told me that during the interrogation another interrogator, Mr. Attmar, showed up. Attmar was one of the few interrogators really famous for his brutality in an already brutal environment. He and his brother both worked at this Khad, and they were of the few interrogators known by their real names. Nobody nicknamed them Lala. While the interrogator, my Lala, was asking these three students questions, Attmar showed up out of the blue. He stood there a few moments and chatted with Lala in their own little language. Attmar asked him, "How are your quails? Are they singing?"

That meant 'have you made them to talk for you, to say the truth? Have you made them to spit out their little secrets?' Lala told him no, that they were not willing to talk. Attmar then took over, telling Fared to tell him the truth: that he *was* a part of that demonstration, unless of course it wasn't true. He promised that if he told the truth, he would be released that very day. "We know you guys were part of that demonstration, just say yes and promise that you will never do such a thing again, and I will let you go."

Fared kept to his story though: "No, we were only the onlookers, we were just going home." Attmar very quickly got upset and started to beat him, just the way they were beating me. But no matter how vicious his strikes were, Fared kept saying that he was simply going home. Attmar then became even more upset, lifted Fared up in the air and slammed him hard into the ground, right down onto the concert floor. He then asked the same questions of the other two. Knowing what would happen to them if they didn't talk, they admitted that they were a part of the demonstrations and promised they would never do so again. Attmar quickly asked them to write everything down, thanked them, and sent them back to the room with promises that soon the two would be released, but told Fared that he would never see the outside world again.

Two days later a guard called Fared out and told him to follow him out of the prison. He was released that day in spite of Attmar's threats.

My interrogation was now a piece of cake. Every day, twice a day, same questions, same answers. My Lala was now a little better with me. He even greeted me when he saw me. Sometimes he asked me about the spelling of his words, even about some of the poets I knew, so we'd talk a little. He was now getting friendlier with me. He truly was becoming a real Lala.

On my eighteenth or nineteenth day, about noon, the guard came and read my name again. The only thing was: I had already been interrogated that day. I immediately began to worry – anything unusual was rarely a good thing. It was too early for another interrogation, typically this would be time for lunch, and then they would come to get me. Either this was something really bad, or I had a visitor. It was not common but it was possible.

I follow the guard to the adjacent building, then into the interrogation room. He opens the door and lets me enter, and boom. I sweat, I begin to faint. I die. It was worse than I had ever imagined. It was my brother, my older brother Khalil. I had put everything on him because he went into hiding. I was expecting him to leave the country, never to be found, but there he was in front of me.

If I still said that everything belonged to him, then he would go through the same hell that I just went through, and if I said no, and admitted that I was lying, everything would be on me. It was obvious I would go through the same hell again and again, until I died a beaten, broken man that only hopefully had not told them everything they wanted to know. Really, my only options were to die or to be responsible for the arrest of thousands. I was going to die, I knew it—for I could not have thousands arrested just because I could not take the beatings anymore. I needed to quarantine myself. Like a disease, the beatings would spread, and then not just me but thousands would find themselves the victim of these thugs. My sister, her friends, everybody was involved. All of my best friends – everybody!

I would be disgraced, and still in prison until I died.

As soon as I entered the room, the skinny weasel with the glasses jumped me and commandingly asked, "Now tell me who is behind the pamphlets!"

It was a split-second decision that felt like an eternity inside: "It is all me, he literally knows nothing about it. He himself is a Parcham sympathizer!!! I was always fighting with him, and thought it would have served him right!!!" The weasel jumped, took my brother by the shirt, and pushed him out of the room, "Take him, take him!" The interrogator was smart and realized that I was coaching him. In a rush he pushed my brother out the door so he could not hear anything else from me. I did what I could, I put my life on the line to get him out, so there was nothing more I could do. I was hoping my brother was smart, that he realized that I was coaching him. That was all of it. I didn't need him anymore, and if he was smart enough he then knew what to say.

If he was not, like the last time, then he would just be sitting in the jail next to me. As soon as my brother was pushed out of the room that skinny guy shouted. "Tell me, if everything belongs to you, then why did you lie all this time?" I shouted back, "What would you be doing if you were in my place!" Now I know the time for being shy is gone. He is not alone, all of my interrogators are there. But he is running the show. He jumps again, this time towards me, takes me by the shoulders and shakes me. He shakes me as hard as he can. "Tell me who are you, and tell me everything if you want to live!" This dirty creature thinks that I am stupid. He could never wring the truth from me.

I knew the only chance I had for survival was not to tell him anything, but in a way that he did not realize it. The only way I could live was to keep my secrets, but convince him that I was not trying to be a hero. To convince him that I was not a tough guy, honestly cooperating, and telling him everything. I was not a criminal who killed twenty people and now had to hide the truth, this was not a sin. I was simply a little nineteen-year-old college student who was leading a student association that kept people from getting hurt and wanted to stop the slaughter of our neighbors, and preserve the sanctity of Afghan soil. Yet they believed that this was the worst possible thing you could have done. We were like enemy combatants to them, worth nothing and given less.

Behind his glasses, the eyes of the weasel were filled with anger. If anger had a face that you could see, it would have been grinning that very day deep down inside the center of his eyes. As he got closer to me, I knew that I needed to stand like a man, like myself. I needed to stand like an Afghan man and take it. The problem was that it was easy to say, but hard as hell to do. When they start beating you, the excruciating pain will reduce you to a little child. When he kicks you under the knee with those demonic shoes of his, he will reduce you to a little girl begging him to stop.

I was giving all I had to myself. I simply said, "Stand there Shafie, you will go through it this time too, and if God helps you, you can die as a man: a proud death."

He soon held me from my ears again, yelling "Tell me, and tell me everything." He pushed my chest against the wall with his body weight. "You will be killed in here, don't try to be a champion. I will kill you during this beating and I will bring your mother to watch." That, I knew I could not handle. "I will bring your mother to watch you; I will beat you even as you lie dying. And then, when she pulls her hair in grief, then you can read your poem: *Madaram ber marg betaboot farzandat manal Bash yakdam roze taglil shahedan merasad.*"

"Do you want me to bring your Mom, to sit in here and watch you die? That *is* what you want, isn't it? So she can mourn for you! Cry as we pour your broken body into an open grave." He pushed my chest against the wall harder and held me. Then he slapped me, on the right cheek while he pushed me against the wall with his left arm as hard as he could. Then he let my body go and start slapping me. My face became numb again. I saw my face turn to the left and to the right. Right and left, and left and right. This time though I was able to hold up my face, just as once upon a time I had held up my palms without flinching. If I was going to die, I was going to die with honor.

Inside of my head, every part of me was finally on the same page. Inside I said quietly, "Beat me, beat me motherfucker, you think I'm scared of you? You can kill me during this beating, and I will die standing. I am an Afghan man; I will fight to free my people. Go ahead, beat me, and I will take it all the way until the last breath goes out, all the way to the very peak of what dignity can possibly ever mean."

Believe me, as he began kicking me under the knees, I had never taken it better before that day. I was holding on good. I was not shouting or crying or begging anymore. Only one part of me was shouting... but that part grew louder. In my head I remembered many things, trying to get away from that room, but one thing in particular stood out. I remembered my Quran teacher in the sixth grade. He once proudly told us that a man at the Mosque told him that his wife talked to herself and cried without reason sometimes, that he did not know how to help her. My teacher replied, "Oh, I know what it is."

The man asked him excitedly, "What is it?"

He told him that she had Satan inside her. It was not her crying — it was Satan crying.

"What should we do dear Mullah?" he asked, now terrified.

"Easy, very easy. I can come and kick Satan out from her body, and then, she will be all right." They set a time for it, and the Mullah went to the man's house, they tied the women, and, our teacher said proudly, "Then I placed four ball pens between her fingers and slowly I started pressing her fingers against them. Soon Satan started crying and shouting again, right in my presence. As I pressed more and more, Satan shouted more and more as well. Then, Satan flowed out and the woman fainted."

"What happened next, teacher sir," someone asked curiously.

"She is doing well now; she never cries anymore." I snapped back into the room and suddenly I was living out the same fate. As the interrogator was kicking me under my knees, It was not me, but my Satan shouting for mercy, begging for mercy, without an ounce of care for any such dignity, about my pride and about my manhood. Inside of that screaming, wailing man I stood, steely, with every bit of dignity I had ever had grasped firmly in hand. I snapped away from the pain, from the torture, from everything earthly, and watched my body squeal.

Every time the weasel beat me, he would continue until I went unconscious. Then, he just threw me onto the floor and left me there. Hours later, I would come back to life and my whole body would be in pain. Again, I could no longer turn away from the wall under my own power.

When we were little and my brothers and sisters and I were playing with each other, Mom was always after us to be gentler with one another. "My son, human beings are sometimes harder than rocks, and sometimes softer than flowers. Someone can easily be killed." I wished then that I was that soft flower, one that could more easily perish – why oh why, I thought to myself, was I that fucking stone? I could not figure out what was keeping me alive in there, why dying was so hard? No, back then we did not have a Dr. Kevorkian, and in a heartbeat I would have given him everything I had to take it: my life!

The door opened as I came to. "Wake up," the voice said as I felt the person pushing me with his foot. I played dead once again, but he knows I am already awake; I finally turned my head to see my interrogator. But it was not the skinny guy, nor was it my Lala. It was that other one. He was much nicer than the weasel, and I had a flash of hope that he was perhaps more like my Lala. He had beaten me only when the weasel was there, but never outside of this. From his accent, I knew he was Pashtun and a Khalqi; right now they were not a major part of the government and, whether or not it was related, he was not much interested in beating me.

A couple of times I was in that interrogation room, when they called my roommate Dr. Ferhad. He was his interrogator too. Instead of interrogating him, he would just keep asking him question about Germany, German life, and how he could get a visa to go to there. From his questions, both Dr. Shah and I, we knew that he was thinking about leaving Afghanistan and the politics of Afghanistan all together.

"Up," he told me with a kinder voice, soon helping me up by the shoulder. He knew what had happened to me. He was in the room when the weasel was beating me. He likely saw me pass out from the pain. He told me to go with him, helping me from underneath my shoulder. My mouth was so dried, that I could not even move my tongue, as it stuck to the bottom and top of my mouth when I tried. I asked him to give me some water and allow me to go to the bathroom. He walked with me to the bathroom, and when I came out, had a cup of water in his hand.

As soon as I was done with the water, he started walking. I walked with him. He walked to the corner of the building, I believe it was in the northeast corner, and opened a door. The door opened to a totally new building. The building had rooms only on one side, about four or five of them. The rooms were different in sizes and, again, all the rooms were located on the east side. The building had a smaller yard in the middle. All the rooms had lights, and from the outside they all looked very crowded. There were a few armed guards and a couple unarmed guards sitting on chairs close to the entrance of the two rooms. In the southeast corner of the building I saw an inmate in white Afghani robe (Perahen and Turban) just standing. He was young, around twenty years old. There was another guy in brownish Afghani robes standing within a few feet of another guard. When we got closer to the guard sitting on the chair, my interrogator told him to keep me standing, not to let me go to sleep, and then he left. The guard commanded me to stand, and pointed to a place a few feet away, close to the wall. Slowly I walked to the place I had been given, and stood.

It is really cold. I am shivering like crazy and cannot stand. The guard notices pretty soon at one point that at any moment I will collapse. He looks around, as if he wants to make sure no one is watching him, and gets up. Over he went to a little room, I believe to their office, and when he came back he had a blanket in hand. Then, he said I could sit. Little things like this seemed to happen every so often, as if many people there understood that what was going on was very wrong. It was not like you hear about in stories about

World War II where the Germans all blindly took orders; my Afghan brethren were torn between a rock and a hard place, but still seemed to understand the wrongness of the situation inside of those walls. I wrap myself in that blanket, sit, lean against the wall, and simply allow my body to lose control.

"Hey, wake up. The interrogators are coming. Wake!" I heard somebody say. I open my eyes, it is early morning. The guard asks me to give him the blanket and stand there as if I had been standing all night. I see what he is trying to do. He does not want to get into trouble because of helping me. I very much understand.

Around eight o'clock it was breakfast time. I had missed a couple meals already but more than anything I was so dehydrated. I could barely move my tongue again. I needed a sip of that sweet tea so badly right now. Whenever I got my first cup of tea in those situations, I never knew what to do first: take a sip, hold it tight against my stomach to warm myself with it, or hold some in my mouth to let it moisten. Usually I would sip and hold, sip and hold, until it was all gone.

That first cup of sweet tea after the evening in the yard of the other building was perhaps the best cup of tea I have ever had. As I drank it, I blew on the tea a little to make it cold, so that when I drank, I rained into my mouth. It was painful to chew the nan bread, I had to soak the bread into the tea, to make it soft enough. I knew that no matter the pain, I needed to eat.

Half an hour later the guard came in and called my name. I followed him back to that interrogation room. My Lala was already there, waiting for me. But as I walked in with a lot of difficulty, he gave me a kinder look as he greeted me. I sat there and without saying anything he left. Then, in a few minutes, he came back with a couple pills and some water. I swallowed the pills and after a moment of silence, he gave me a look. He spoke, "Shafie now we know nothing belongs to your brother. We will need you to talk, and to tell us the truth, that is the only way out for you."

While he is talking he is playing with his pen, "I know you cannot stand for long and you will go to waste." He added, "When the boss comes back, there will be a lot of torture. I am not telling you as an interrogator, just as some friendly advice." While he was talking I was trying to calculate what he was saying. I agreed that I would not be able to take these beatings for long. I was thinking of where I could find a better solution. In my head, I sorted through all the ideas I had come up with since the night before. Next, he opened his file and wrote me a question. As usual, he pushed the paper towards me for an answer.

"Who was doing the printing?"

He wanted me to give him the source, the people with the printer. "I don't know them," I responded.

He read the answer, took a little time, and wrote again, "Who are your connections?"

His questions were not new, they were almost the same, and I answered the same way. He did not beat me, in fact, I felt that he was trying to be helpful. I did not trust him, but I took it kindly. Close to lunchtime he left, and after lunch he came back. A couple hours later he left again. Then, after dinner, around nine o'clock, the weasel crawled back out of his hole. He was with the nighttime interrogator, the man who we all knew wanted out of the country, and had Germany deep within his eyes in that place where the weasel only had rage.

As he entered I saw he was already upset. The first look he gave me was very bad, as he slid his files onto the table. He sat there, giving me another look, and simply asked, "Are you ready to talk, or do you really want me to bring your mother in?" He picked up right where he'd left off the other night. He had indeed given me something to think about: it was not at all common to bring someone's mother to see her son being tortured, or to torture a mother or a sister or wife to break the will of a man, but it had happened before. A few months ago, the Khalqis were doing such things, but so far this new government was trying to prove that they were different than the Khalqis. It was more than likely that he was not going to bring in my mother, that it was just a bluff, but you could never tell what those communists really thought the next best move could be.

The weasel never wrote his questions down. His questions were always verbal, and always short. You could see he actually enjoyed the torture. He repeated himself again, "Tell me who is printing the pamphlets, and tell me, who are your connections?"

"Okay I will tell you. I'll talk," I tell him. He is not surprised at all, he probably saw this a lot. He had probably broken a lot of proud men. He knew how much a human could take.

"Good, this is good. But you need to know that I know when people lie. Even last time, I knew you were lying."

He looked for me to respond. "No, I will not lie. I will tell you everything I know."

I tell him that I don't know a lot of people, but since I am a writer, someone approached me to write their anti-government papers. Unfortunately, I had accepted, but after I gave them a copy of the manuscript for a pamphlet I changed my mind and I asked them not to use my manuscript. The copy I had, I put in the fireplace.

"Do you want me to believe this?" he asked.

"Yes, this is the truth," he gave me a different kind of look, as if he were analyzing my response like a robot.

"Well good, then give me their names," he responded.

"There are two of them. One is Najib and one is Hamid."

With the same look, he followed up: "Where do they live?"

"I don't know exactly where, but I think they live in Shahr-e-naw," I said.

He asked me another question, "How did you know them?"

"From the university."

"How did you meet them?"

I told him that one day I was returning a book at the university library, a Maulana Jalalludin Ghazaliat, and he was behind me. As I was returning the book he started talking with me. When he realized that I was a writer, he asked me if he could see me another day, as he had questions about Maulana. When we met, he had his friend Najib with him. A few days later they invited me for a cup of tea and asked me if I could help them with their pamphlets. "Which political organization they belong to?" the weasel asked.

I answered, "they were with the Kabul University student associations."

The weasel asked me where they could be found, and I said, "At the University. They are engineering students."

But he did not want to wait until the following day, "No, tonight. Give me an address."

I told him that I didn't know. He stood up. "I know you know where they live. You need to tell me," he said. He came right at me, with his finger pointing at me to stand up. He held me by the ears and began slapping me. He slapped me hard, and kept telling me to take him to their house.

To be honest, I didn't know where Hamid lived, but I knew exactly where Najib lived, though I was not sure when I should tell him. Both Najib and Hamid had already left Afghanistan two weeks prior to my arrest. In those days when people left Afghanistan they could not leave legally, especially young men: they all escaped Afghanistan illegally to Pakistan or Iran, and from there they either got a visa to some European country or the United States, or they just flew there with a fake visa and applied for political asylum, which they could easily get. So, for the weasel to prove that I was lying was impossible, but that was not important. I wanted him to buy what I was telling him. I wanted him to beat me good; I wanted him to spit it out of me. That way he might accept that the information I was giving was the truth, that he had forced it out of me. That way if he suspected it was only false information, the memory of the beating would redirect his thoughts. He needed to feel as if he had succeeded at a hard fought game and not feel as if this was a suspicious change of heart.

He beat me like the night before. He kicked me like that night, he hit my head one, two, three, four... and I crack. I shout, "I know, I know where they live."

He stopped "Where?"

I reply with blood dripping from my lips that "Hamid lives in Shah-e-Naw. I don't know exactly but I can describe it for you."

"Forget about descriptions, you can just take me there." he asked.

"Yes!" I yell.

He commands my other interrogator to get him a couple jeeps with some armed personnel. They quickly put me in the back of a jeep and take me to Shahr-e-Naw.

From where I was being held it was probably a twenty minute drive. Once in the area he asked me how to get there, and I told him that I had been in their house only once, so I didn't know exactly how. I told him that if he took us to the park's theater, I would be able to find it more easily. They pulled into the parking lot of the Park Theater and he asked me again which way it was. I replied that I thought it was that way and pointed my hand, then that way for a couple of hours. Kabul streets are dark at night, and I used that as an excuse. For a couple hours I enjoyed the outside world, the free people and their midnight strolls, until they had finally had enough and brought me back. They took me again to the same place as the night before and told the guard not to let me sleep.

The guard again is an angel. He knows that I am not able to stand. A little later, again he brings me a blanket and tells me I can sit. As soon as I do, I instantly fall asleep.

The next morning after breakfast I was taken again for interrogation with my Lala. That day his questions were about Najib and Hamid, their descriptions, their addresses, their behavior, their political views, their connections, their Dads' names, who their brothers were, and anything about any of their friends. Were they armed? Did they have weapons training? He asked me a lot until lunchtime. He then let me have my lunch, before returning for the entire afternoon of the same questions.

At about five pm they put me in the jeep again and took me to Shah-e-naw. Because I told them that Najib and Hamid sometimes came to the park for a walk, we sat there and waited. The park was one of the most popular parks in Kabul, where lots of teenagers used to hang out before the communist coup just to flirt. It was still crowded with boys and girls, but not like before. People were too fearful to stay outside very late. The hope was that I either saw them there or better remembered the route to their homes. Again I took them for a joyride. The outside world was stunning to me, I enjoyed every minute of it. I just kept telling them, make a right here, and make a left there, and I took in the world as if I had just been born. Then, as we cross a busy intersection, I saw something that made me duck... it was Husnia Osman.

Husnia was my classmate at Kabul University. She was also a television broadcaster at Afghan TV. It was two years now that Afghanistan had a TV station, though it was run by the government. Husnia was a very intelligent girl, and absolutely beautiful. She was probably one of the ten most beautiful girls at all of Kabul

University. She was also a very close friend of mine. I was very worried; I didn't want her, or anyone else to see me in that jeep. Those jeeps were known as being owned by Afghan central service. If someone saw me in that jeep, soon there would be a rumor about me that I was cooperating with the Khad, and all of my friends would be concerned. In fact, half of my classmates were members of our associations, and they would all be worried that their arrests were imminent.

It was around 10 pm, when we return to the Khad. The skinny weasel gave the guards instructions as soon as we were back, then left. The guards then took me to the same building where I had spent that last two nights. This time they just took me into one of the rooms. As I got in, my suspicions of the crowdedness of the rooms were all found to be quite correct. There were about twenty-five people in a room approximately twenty by twenty-five feet. The room was crowded with little mattresses, blankets, and pillows. Some of the people were already asleep, some were awake.

I said hello and entered the room, soon recognizing a few familiar faces. These were the ones that I saw standing outside the first night, when I was forced to stand, as the group of us were not allowed to sleep. They both recognized me too. As I looked at one, he moved himself a little bit to make some room for me, and over I went. As I sit, again we greet each other. He asks me how I am. In America if you ask someone, 'how are you doing?' the answer will differ from time to time. Some may say 'good', some might say 'excellent', some might say that they are doing terrible, or whatever fits their situation, but in Afghanistan if you ask even a very ill person that can barely walk, he will say "Shukour Khobhastom (thanks to god, I am doing good)."

A moment later he asks my name. "Shafie," I reply.

"Are you a student?" he asks afterwards. I tell him yes, and then ask his name and what he did on the outside. He tells me that his name is Nazeer Gul, a Kabul University student in the Faculty of Economics. He asks me why I was arrested, and just like always I say, "I don't know."

When I asked him in return, he said "I am a member of Afghan Melat," a very small racist Pashtun organization. He asked me about my interrogation and if they had made me to talk yet. I told him that I did not have anything important to say, but that yes, yes I told them what I knew. Then I asked him the same question and he told me that for a couple weeks he resisted, and that he endured a lot of torture, but finally they injected him with some kind of chemical. After that he was done, he was unable to control what he said, and told them everything.

It became very clear that just not talking had never been an option. It also became apparent that they must have enjoyed the torture in some way, for if they could simply do one injection and get what they wanted, why would they not do it on day one? It became clear that my level of terror was nowhere where it needed to be. Though one never did know who was being honest about what in there, and the chemical story seemed utterly fantastical. I wanted to dig a little deeper, "Did you give them the names of your connections?"

"Yes," he replied.

That made me even more curious. "Are they being arrested?"

"Yes, my whole group is being arrested," he said. I was so unsure about what he was saying. I knew that if he was telling me the truth and that his whole group was being arrested that meant that yes he had given them information. One still couldn't be sure. The answers to my questions made me worry even more. What if they really had injected him with something, so that he lost control over his brain, finding it cracked open for the weasel and his breed to feed upon.

The whole night long I thought about Nazergul and that injection. If this chemical really existed, then why had they not injected me with it yet I asked myself. Or, maybe they had, I did not remember... After the level of torture I had experienced, the pain I had been through, I had to suspect that he had simply had the information beaten out of him, and was embarrassed – making up excuses. I tried to figure out what to do no matter whether he was telling the truth or not. Should I just make it easy on myself and tell them whatever I knew, or should I still resist? We Afghans were a very simple people, but these Russians were highly educated with really advanced technology. The reputation of the Red Army gave gravity to what Nazergul had said. But I still decided that I would not tell them anything. If they injected me with something to extract the information out of me then I would not feel guilty, because in that case it would not be me that provided it. Or rather, according to my Quran teacher, they would take nothing from me, they would take only from my Satan!

It was breakfast time soon enough. Then, as usual, I needed to follow a guard to the next building for interrogation. Lala was already there. He greeted me and asked me to have a seat. Even during this second round of interrogation, Lala did not change his relationship with me. Lala, during the second round of torture, had not beaten me at all. By the Khad standard, you could say he was really friendly with me. Twice a day he asked me questions and I would give him answers, and it felt like he was just trying to do his job. He was not there to determine any deeper truths about the situation.

As I sat Lala, who was busy looking at the file, asked me once again about my Hamid and Najib descriptions. I gave him as much as possible, and then he picked something from the files and showed it to me. "Do you know this guy?" he asked.

"Yes I know him, he is Hamid," I tell him. Then he put the picture back, writing something down, and then showed me another picture.

"Do you know him?"

"Yes, this is Najib." That told me that they had already stormed their houses. Their poor families, how scared they probably were when a bunch of armed people stormed their homes. They probably had no idea what was going on. My Lala shook his head and told me they had already escaped: that they were in Germany now. "Are they?" I said, acting as surprised as could be.

I knew that the upcoming night would bring the weasel back to this same cell, with that same rage in his eyes. He was the important guy, he was the boss. If he accepted that Najib and Hamid were my connections, especially if he accepted that they had used me to write the pamphlets, then I believed that he might not see any reason to press me further. I was not expecting them to think that I was innocent , I am sure they knew that I had been an active person in anti-government activities, but once they accepted that I was a lower ranking member, I believed they would not see any reasons to beat me to death. This new government really was trying to convince the Afghans that they were better than the Khalqis, which they really were. Although I was going through hell, only a few months ago, for the same allegations, they would have stormed my house and arrested not only me but my whole family. I would be dead, as would my two brothers.

At 6pm my Lala was done with me, and told the guard to take me to the room where Nazergul was. I followed the guard to that same room. Once inside I quickly saw that the other guy who stood outside on that first night, not Nazergul but the other one, was there. He was a bit shorter than Nazergul, but very athletic. He had a white *peran tunban* robe. He too made a little room for me. I had more sympathy for him and Nazergul in this room, because of our common plight those two evenings. While greeting a few others within close proximity to me, I sat silently for a while waiting to see if the man asked my name, or wanted to know about my interrogations. He simply sat there quietly though and did not say a word.

Around eight o'clock dinner was served. While eating I asked the man his name, to which he replied "Shokoor". I asked him if he was a student, and he answered that he was in law at Kabul University. He did not ask me anything in return. I tried hard to open up a conversation with him, to see if he knew anything about this chemical Nazergul had spoken to me about. I wanted to see if he also knew about it, but I saw he was not ready to talk. I fully understood.

Tomorrow was the same for me. I was taken to the same room for interrogation and asked similar questions. My interrogation after lunch was a shorter one. In fact, Lala wanted to just chat with me to a certain extent. Nothing in writing. I guess he was so used to me now, he was just a little curious about what else was underneath my facade.

After the interrogation he told the guard to take me to the first housing quarters where I had met my younger brother. I followed the guard back to that building, and entered the crowded yard. The guard took me to the same room, though everybody else was outside. The room was empty. I left the room too, as soon as the guard had left.

First, I see Dr. Ferhad, who greets me as if we were brothers. All the other guys from the room come and greet me one by one. I then see my younger brother walking towards me too. It was a pleasure to see him, but at the same time… my heart broke to see that they still had not let him go. I asked him about our older brother to see if he had seen him, but he had not. Nervously he asks me the same, as he still did not know that he was also arrested. I told him about it, and his cheeks lost their color. He knew that made it even harder for Mom and at the same time understood that his arrest affected my interrogations quite severely. But once again I lied a bit to protect him from the truth, and to make him feel better about the news.

Still, everyday, as usual, twice a day, they took me for interrogation. Now most of it was just Lala and I having a conversation. When I was done with the interrogation, I was soon back in the room. Unlike the other more crowded rooms with those that appeared to have been broken for more serious offenses, we could secretly talk, joke, and try to make the best out of a bad situation. We were very lucky that Dagerwal was in our room. His chess set provided a great deal of entertainment. I was able to learn and get quite good at it, as I helped my roommates with their interrogations too. Still, I was always wary that one of them might be a spy.

That summer was very hot, I remember. Having twelve people in one small room didn't help any. This was especially true during the afternoon, as our room was among the few rooms located at the east side of the building, when the afternoon sun shone directly into our faces. The other problem was that this little room had only one window and one that could not be opened. We had to keep the door half closed though, as sometimes the interrogators check to see if we are talking to each other when it was not allowed to really do so. On the few days I did not have a second interrogation, I would try to just sleep through it.

One afternoon I was in a deep sleep when I began dreaming that someone, like a small child, was crying. I went forward trying to see who it was, but I could not. The crying continued until I finally woke up, but still, I heard that cry. I realized suddenly that it was not just a dream. I opened my eyes to see my roommates are all very quiet and nervous. Turning my head to the other direction, I tried to see what was making them so nervous. I didn't see anyone, but I still heard their cry. I sat, then moved myself closer to the door, which was half way shut, to see who was there.

Eventually I make out a little body, sitting on the threshold with his back towards us. From his body size I could tell he was too young to be in a place like this, perhaps ten to twelve years old. He had a *peran tunban* robe and a little round hat. Usually the boys in urban Kabul find hats have fallen out of fashion, so I determined that he must have been from rural Kabul. So he was likely one of those poor little Afghan boys that did not go to school, as they were needed by their families to work. We didn't have a lot of them in those days. They were very limited in numbers and usually belonged to Hazara families. The Hazara were one of the minorities in Afghanistan, with a distinct oriental look. They were all Muslims, but we treated them almost like the Sikh. The Hazara were always treated with a very special disrespect, even though they were Muslims just like us.

It broke my heart to see a little child in that fearful detention center. My roommates told me that they had tried to calm him down, but nothing worked. Since the boy was not inside the room they were not able to do more, because they did not want the spies to see them helping another inmate.

I slid a little closer to the door, within a foot from him, and started talking to him. "Are you okay?" I asked. He did not answer me. "Are you missing your Mom and Dad?" He still did not reply. "Have they beaten you a lot?" No answer. I got a little closer and started rubbing his shoulders, but still there was no result. For twenty minutes nothing helped, but finally he turned his face towards me and told me that he was crying because they tortured him a lot to give them the name of his connections, and though he did not, his other little friend could not take the torture anymore and had given up.

Some student at Kabul University had given these two little boys, street vendors that carried little wooden displays on their shoulders to sell gum, candy, and single cigarettes to bring home the family living, some anti-government pamphlets to spread at the University. Most likely, it had been someone from my organization. This little boy was not crying because he was beaten to within an inch of his life. He was not crying because he was away from his home, sitting in prison. He was not crying because he was perhaps his family's only breadwinner, and his family might suffer without him. He was crying because his other little friend had not resisted to the death, and had given the names of a few students... and he was worried that now they would be caught.

I am stunned. I don't know if I should just continue to rub his back and calm him down, or if I should ask him to rub my back and calm me down. I was confused between treating this little illiterate boy who could never dream of going to university, who had been thrust in here and tortured for a cause I began, like a child, or like a hero. I thought that I was patriot until that moment. I thought I was a hero. I thought that I was a tough guy, but to look at this ten-year-old boy and his concerns, his loyalty, his pride, and his dignity... everything changed for me.

The Pashtun dominated government had always made it even harder for little Hazara kids like him to even be able to go to school. In the government, there were almost no Hazara position the higher ranks, nor were there any in the upper ranks of the military. Hazaras were one of the most smart and hard working peoples in Afghanistan who might be capable of leading Afghanistan to become one of the world's best countries, yet the discrimination against them ensures they do only the hard physical work that no one else wants to do in the country. I don't know what I should write about him, because even in my own language of Dari I am not able to write enough about him, now in English I am already ten thousand words short. His little figure coming out of my dream was like a holy leaf falling from the sky gently towards the ground, drifting on the winds without complaint. As I rubbed his back, I felt hot tears rolling over my face.

It was now close to the sixth week of my detention. My Lala called me only one time this week, where we sat and talked about all kinds of things. Everything he asked me was something that just came into his mind at the moment. My nighttime interrogations had completely stopped, and I had not seen the weasel in a very long time. I felt that I had recovered a great deal, as much in my mind as it was in body. I was not happy to be in detention, but I thanked God that so far I was still living and had not given any names.

I remember another very hot night. The room felt far too small for twelve people, even more so than usual. A few of our roommates were already asleep, a few just deep in thought. I and a few other roommates were watching Dagerwal and another roommate playing chess. The door then opened and a guard read my name. He asked me to follow him to the interrogation room. My heart began to pound, as I envisioned it starting all over again. I was so happy that my interrogation was coming to an end, but now they were asking me back to that same room in the middle of the night. Somebody else must have been caught, was all I could think.

There before me was the weasel again. Before him was my file. He asked me to sit. He had beaten me so much that at this point that he did not have to torture me anymore; just to look at him hurt my very soul. I quietly sat and waited to see what was going on.

"I just called to tell you that your file has been completed, and that soon you will be sent to Policharki Jail to await your trail."

You could not measure my happiness at that moment with a ten foot pole. I wanted to start jumping up and down. This man I had grown to hate was, for a moment, my best friend in the entire world. But I controlled my emotions, as I believed showing any kind of emotion could be costly, as an innocent man would not jump up and down so much at the news of being sent to prison. "Others faint, and he is dancing?" that sort of thing. I asked him sadly for more information. He told me that as soon as they could, they would send papers to my cell at Policharki, explaining to me what I had been charged with. Then it would be up to me to write for my own defense, and on a designated date, I would be sent to the revolutionary court for a judge to listen and decide my fate.

He then sent me back to my room. My roommates were trying to give me support, telling me that it was okay, and that the judge may well set me free… but inside I was already dancing as if I were a free man again.

In my bed I rethought each of my interrogations. For close to seven weeks, it was hellish. But my anger felt some relief that night. In many ways I was not so upset anymore. I knew they had beaten me severely, but being beaten in Afghanistan was not so unusual. The beatings of kids start at a very young age. That is the way it is: our dads work really hard to earn a living for us, a little bread, shelter, a pair of clothes a year... that is how far someone's dream can fly. If you have that, you are rich. Our dads work really hard to provide us with that. Our fathers, however, had no other provision for pleasure in their own lives but for sex.

Of course more sex meant more kids, as no contraception was ever used: men and women thought that the more kids they brought into the world the better it was for Islam. They believed that if you brought more kids into the world one need not worry, for God would feed them, as it was not you that provided food for these kids, it was God. They believed that every morning God sent his angels to all the houses and they decided what to bring to fill your stomachs, like some kind of Santa Claus. If you prayed more and if you were a pure believer in Muhammad, your share would be more, otherwise it would be less.

Based on this mentality, nobody cared about condoms anyways, even if they found out about them—using it would only be detrimental to their true goal in life and the real goal of sex for them. As a result, every year or so a child is born. Usually six to eight children was common. By then the mothers and fathers were simply worn out. They had no time to spend with the kids. They were so worn out that they could not even listen to the noises of their kids when they played. The Dad was the first one who beats you, and soon you get used to it.

In Afghanistan people think that kids are like little animals - that they don't understand anything but beatings. Generation after generation, that was the way it had always been. Your mother could beat you too, but not like your dad could. You always had something in common with your mom, in addition to the fact that your mom had something in common with you. She was simply overwhelmed, every day, by your father. Treated forcefully, often beaten. For something as small as your mother putting some extra salt in the food, your dad could begin to slap her. That, I always found, created a bond between mother and child, making mothers nicer and giving them a deep feeling of dissatisfaction and sympathy when your father came after you; a feeling you could see in their eyes.

But unfortunately, fathers had to be fathers, and that meant being tough on their kids. It was not that many of them really wanted to beat their kids, but they truly believed they had to. The second person that beats you is your Mullah. I was so happy that we were never sent to the Mosque, but the majority of people felt obligated to send their kids there to learn the Quran and other religious stuff. Your Mullah had the same right as your dad. He, the Mullah, was also used to this culture of beatings, and he would not hesitate. Especially because he often truly believed that he was teaching you God's words, and that if you did not pay attention you were no better than Satan himself. He would beat you like the weasel did, and no one would ask him why.

These kinds of rights created a huge problem with sexual moles-tation among the Mullahs in Afghanistan. In Islamic societies men and women are separated, forbidden to be together, but men have boys within their reach. I believe that this was why a lot of boys in Afghanistan were the victim of child molestation, and believe me a lot of it came from the Mullahs and Talibs - the Mullah's underlings. Most of the sexual molestations went unnoticed though, because the little kids were afraid to tell others. If you were molested in Afghanistan, you are disgraced. From that day forth you can no longer be a normal member of the society. People will punish you too if you are a victim of rape or molestation.

They expect you to take a knife and slaughter the molester; oth-erwise you were seen as a coward and deserve to be punished fur-ther, by others too. Much of this punishment comes in the form of additional sexual molestation. How can a little boy take a knife and kill a Mullah or Talib, accusing them of rape, when the Mullahs held such reverence in society? Over centuries this has happened so often, that now in parts of Afghanistan molestation of children has simply become culturally acceptable. I remember when I was in the sixth grade, there was a kid in our school and somehow the other kids found out that he had been molested. The other kids simply started to prey on him. It became so severe that every day at recess and at the end of the school day, a gang of a hundred kids were waiting at the school gate for him. As soon as he was there, the flock of little kids charged at him and tried to shove their little fingers up his ass. It became such a problem that our principal had to send one of the school clerks, a really strong man, to give the little boy protection, and take him home. I remember that even then as he was walking he was shrinking down and keeping his briefcase behind his backside to protect himself.

The third person that beats you is your teacher, especially the Quran teachers and the Pashto language teachers as I said before. Although Pashtuns are only about 25 % of the people of Afghanistan, and Pashto is spoken by probably only 20% of Afghans on a constant base, it was still taught in schools as our second language. The Pashto teachers were particularly mean.

This was the atmosphere in which Afghan kids were raised. From childhood we learned to obey our Dad and the Mullah and the teachers. Our Pashto teachers beat us largely because they were racist too, but even in that case we needed to respect and obey them. At a very young age we learned that our Dad was always right. White milk is black if our Dad says it's black, or our Quran teacher or our Pashto teachers.

There were various ways to punish the students. The easiest and most common was used by my teacher Amina Jan, was to use a half inch by three foot switch cut fresh from a tree. The strike on the palms of your hands was usually delivered with as much power as your teacher could muster. If they wanted to punish you a little more, they would strike at the back of your hands. A little more painful than that was when they would strike at the tip of your fingers. Any ten year old child would wince, and never forget that pain for the rest of their lives. Others would use four pens and place them one by one between your fingers, then start pressing your fingers against the pens. The students simply thought of it as common, that nothing was wrong.

That is why Afghanistan and the majority of the Islamic societies are the perfect environment to incubate and raise the best communists and the best Taliban. We are used to accepting things without asking questions, and once we are grownups, we kill the people that challenge us. Everybody needs to obey us, because we are always right, just like our Quran teachers were. That is why the Afghan communists took to the Communism that was most extreme by itself to an extreme that people around the world where appalled by in the first place. We Afghans disgraced Communism and sent it to the graveyard in many ways. Believe me, if Islam did not have such deep roots in our people, Islam also could have been sent to the graveyard just for what our Mujahideen did, but who knows.

As I am lying there in the cell, I think about my interrogation, about the glasses perched on the nose of the weasel, about all the torture, and I feel a sense of relief. Somehow my heart is trying to move forward. I was right there on the mattress, with the bed bugs nipping at my flesh over and over again, and the heat of the night overtaking me, trying to forgive and to forget. "I don't know what I would have done to my interrogator if I was his interrogator," I thought, as I argued against my unforgiving side.

A few days later, at around six in the afternoon, the guards brought a long list and started reading our names. Hundreds of people from the detention center's different buildings were being loaded into buses, escorted by armed guards in the jeeps. We were being shipped to Policharki.

Policharki jail was about an hour's drive from the center of Kabul. It was a massive prison on the outskirts of the city built with Soviet money just a few years before the invasion. It was almost as though the Russians had planned to take Afghanistan long before the communists here first took power. The construction finished just before the pro-Soviet coup, and the communists were the first to start using the facility. The jail was enormous, far too large for the city of Kabul during a time of more regular, fair law and order. The official capacity was perhaps five thousand prisoners, but as it was at the Khad, the building was packed far, far over capacity.

When construction of it began during the Daoud regime, the people of Afghanistan were already suspicious, though they had no idea what was about to befall them. The towering prison was built right under their noses, and as people went by they were continuously perplexed: why a giant prison, why not a badly needed hospital, or housing facility, or even a university? In a nation that did not have more than few thousand inmates in the whole country, the logic behind a prison that could be packed with over 20,000 -30,000 people, if necessary, just wasn't there. It was a topic of debate. People wondered.

When the jail was completed immediately before the coup and the communist regime was the first one to use it, the rumor spread very quickly that the Russians had always intended it as a vehicle of oppression and torture. A slowly built monolith gathering strength for war right under our noses. A place away from public eyes where the innocent could scream as loudly as the human voice was able to without alerting a soul to the nightmare of anguish bestowed upon them for daring to not simply fall into line.

This jail had the worst reputation in Afghanistan at the start of the invasion. However, the national memory of Policharki casts a far longer, haunting shadow over the country. Tens of thousands of people vanished behind those gargantuan walls as if they had never existed at all. Although the new government had put a nicer face on its more public actions, the firmness of the foundation of their promise to do better by the people was as corrupt as the people who made it. The day I was shipped to Policharki, I was but one of hundreds crated off to this place, one of the darkest corners of the world. As word returned to the families of the jailed, a chill unlike any other would spread.

Once in front of the gate I look up into the prison like never before—this is a military fortress of epic proportions, the kind that would have made ancient armies tremble. Uncommon to our country, the prison was surrounded by huge rock walls three times higher than the average man. The rod iron gate was surrounded by dozens of armed guards, both inside and out. The transport waited about ten minutes while the guards looked over the papers from the officials taking us there before they opened the gate for us to allow the buses to move inside the perimeter.

As soon as we were inside, there were walls inside the walls, and the stone of the exterior walls was slowly replaced by stark concrete. The interior was constructed out of the grayest of cement, each enclosure with its own high walls and iron gates: as if this were a place of many prisons within prisons, within prisons. A labyrinth of pain, filled with humans guarded only by their torturers. It was an eighth of a mile further into this complex before the bus stopped.

After a few moments, guards boarded the bus and requested that we exit and form a straight line. They read each of our names and had us enter the gates of hell one by one.

Inside the perimeter was yet another great three story building made of concrete. The building again had its own gate and guards armed to the teeth. They divided us into several groups and then escorted us group by group inside the building. As we entered, a 400 by 18 foot tunnel with rooms on both sides opened before us. There was no sun. What little light that came from the light bulbs, weakened with age, carved out the silhouettes of men kept inside each cage. One guard escorted our group, composed of only high-school and university students, all the way to the end of the hall. At the very end another guard with a tangle of keys hanging from his belt unlocked the room's own gate and instructed us to enter.

As we did so, I saw that all the inmates in the room were young students from Kabul University. I saw my friend Shukor waving to me, my inmate from the Khad with the white robe. As I approach him he gave me a hug. We simply stood there, holding each other as tightly as possible, as if we were blood brothers that had not seen each other in a very long time. He introduced me to another boy, his younger brother Aziz, from the science faculty. Aziz was far taller than Shukor with an extremely athletic build.

As we began to talk I felt a hand rubbing my back: another friend, Mustafa Rawani, a classmate from university. Soon I saw another smiling face: Wasi, a good friend from the eighth grade. He was an engineering student now. Then another friend, one of my best, Baser Hakimie: a member of our association. I quickly learned that out of 120 people in our room built for forty; at least twenty were good friends. As our life paths all crossed here in this sordid nexus, I forgot for a while where we were. The shock, the environment, it all brought a sense of community at first – as if it was just a large party. For a moment I felt as if it was a brother's wedding, surrounding me with family.

They made room for a bed for me and asked the guards for a pillow, mattress, and blanket. This room was once again filled with beds exactly two feet by six feet, laid on the concrete floor, side by side, with but six inches of space between them. As if I were still at some party, they brought me tea. "How did you make this?" I asked, surprised. Everybody laughed, as Shukor explained to me that some of the prisoners had jerry-rigged some kind of electric water heater, that could boil a gallon of water in just a few minutes.

The heater was made of two aluminum cans and some wires from the window screen. As I began drinking my tea, someone then offered me a cookie, then someone else offered me some candy. Upon handing it to me, they also let me know that each Friday was Paywaze day: a day when a close relative was able to visit you. The visit could not be in person however, they simply allowed them to send you a short letter to be delivered by a soldier to you from the outside. You could then write something short in return and send it back to them as they waited outside the walls. At the same time they could send you a little money, some food, or a fresh, clean pair of cloths. You could send back your clothing to be washed by your family in return.

The group peppered me with questions about my interrogation and the reason I had been arrested, but I was again overly cautious. I had a lot of stories to share, some good, some bad, but one could never tell exactly who was listening. It would have been easy enough to just relax in this room of likeminded men and tell the story of founding the first anti-government student association after the coup, about the pamphlets, about leading a secret organization of thousands... but I knew, even here, that such words could bring death. Others were more open, but I had a lot to think about: my friends, the associations, my family. There were many people outside those walls relying on my silence.

The early morning loud azan – our prayer call – wakes me. It amazes me. In the Khad, there was no Azan and if we prayed, we all did so out of sight from the interrogators. During the reign of the Khalqis, even outside of the jail people were fearful of praying openly. It is perhaps a part of the story I have not shared with you yet. Even more precious than our hope and daily life, they had robbed us of our ability to share our struggles with God.

The population had deep fears that they would be targeted just for going to Mosques for prayer, something that had been done five times a day for over a thousand years. For the Khalqis, even going to Mosque was an anti-government action that could result in having you thrown in jail. It appeared that the new government had learned that there were some things nobody would turn a blind eye to, even at the risk of slaughter. But the shock of hearing that Azan made me uncertain as to whether to rise or not.

We'd only been asleep a few hours. I sat up cautiously to see what the others would do. Only about ten people were preparing for the morning prayers, so uncertain of my position, I lay back down and went to sleep. In Kabul the majority of young kids did not do their prayers or go to the mosque fife times a day except in the month of Ramadan. Even then, not all of them did all five prayers a day.

By ten or eleven everybody was awake and ready to go outside. I could barely wait to see who else was in there. The room made tea and breakfast for itself. Shukor leaned over to me as it was prepared to warn me about the terrible food the prison staff tried to give us. They gave each prisoner a loaf of bread per day, but not Afghani flat bread. The bread came in thick fat pieces about 2 inches thick. It was Russian bread baked in the government bakeries, sent in to feed the foreign prisoners. Its taste was sour, with a dark brown color. At lunch one of the worst rice dishes I ever had come across was served, and for dinner they prepared a shourba with one potato and a very small piece of meat bobbing across a pot of broth-less hot water. Each pot, with a single potato and single piece of meat, was to feed ten people. I told them about the food at the Khad, and they were amazed. Many of them began to wish out loud that they could be moved there, but they did not know at what price they would be eating that excellent food!

While I was eating my breakfast I began thinking about my older brother. I knew my younger brother still was in the Khad, but I wanted to see if my older one had been transferred here. Once the entire room had eaten their bread, we were able to leave. The outside yard was huge, about two acres. As we went outside I soon saw a few more of my roommates from Khad. Dr. Shah was one of the first, and I quickly walked over to him. We hugged each other as hard as we could. As we greeted each other, I saw Alimohamad and his friend Sadeq. I then saw Dagerwal, as more and more people came to see me again and again.

I let Shukor and all my new roommates go and I stayed with my previous roommates. The building was located right in the center of the yard, so we began walking around the building. The more I walked, the more people I saw who knew me from the outside. But the one person I could not find was my older brother; I had not seen or heard of my older brother. I just hoped that it was a sign of his release.

"Doctor Shafie," they had begun to call me as, though I was not yet a doctor, just being in medical school was a wonder for many of them, "this Friday, hopefully your Paywaze will show up," Dagerwal said to me as I talked about it. My new title originated at the Khad, when they asked me about my career. Soon they insisted on calling me Dr. Shafie, although it thoroughly embarrassed me every time.

If I asked them not to, but my friends would just say, "Why not, you will soon be a doctor, no?" In Afghanistan you just have to let a lot of things like that go, as it is very easy to offend somebody by getting firm with them—ironically, considering the tale of harsh punishment and torture I have just shared.

"My Mom does not yet know that I am in Policharki," I answered.

"She will soon find out. Most of these mothers," he told me, "Go to the Khad every day to find out about their sons. As soon as you are sent here, they will know."

"We will see," I replied.

After three days it was Friday. Everyone was up early, as all the kids became excited at who would "visit" them and what they might bring. The energy was electric, and you could see enthusiastic looks on their faces like I had never seen before – at least on some of them. Especially as all there was to buy in the prison from the small canteen, was a few cans of Russian fish, some eggs, and other things that outside these walls no university student would jump for joy over.

Around eight o'clock a soldier with a packet came into the room and read someone's name. The soldier handed the note to the person as they approached him, allowing him to read it. Right there in front of the soldier, the boy wrote that "Yes, he was okay, and received the things sent with the letter" and then handed the soldier his clothes. As soon as the soldier left everybody congratulated him, and joked,

"Don't forget about us when you eat that good food." Soon though, we were bombarded with soldiers coming and going, as almost everybody got a Paywaze. The rest of the world may have been turning a blind eye to us, but our families never forgot us... well, I hoped that the same would be true for me, but I did not know.

Hour after hour, each time a soldier entered I felt myself perk up, but time and time again he read somebody else's name. My anxiety built over time, as doubts filled my mind. By the time the last soldier entered, I knew that nobody had come to visit me. Although I had all the friends in the world in there, there was nobody outside those walls that knew, I thought. Yet in our room, there is now an actual party. Food, fruit, everything I had not had in months, was being shared. I ate, and I smiled, but I worried.

Later in the day Dr. Shah showed up and invited me to go to his room and have an early dinner with him. It was another thing they allowed us to do - go into different rooms as long as they were on the same floor. Dr. Shah belonged to a rich family, and boy did they send him a large dish of excellent palaw. I was already full, but I didn't mind at all. I stuffed myself like Thanksgiving.

Suddenly, in the middle of everything, another soldier came to the door. He lifted up a note and read a name aloud "Shafie walad-e-Sayed Aulliah." My heart leapt! The people in the room showed pointed at me, and he handed me a letter.

It was from my mother and I remember it well... "*Bachem Khoda konad khoob bashy. Amroz Khad raftum, aunha guftan to ra enja entiqal dadan. Delem preshan hast, Jan mother , brem naweshta ko.*" It read: 'My dear son, I pray that you are doing good. I went to Khad today, and they told me that you have been transferred to Policharki. I am so worried my dear, please let me know." She added that Khalil Jan and Rahmath Jan wanted to say hello.

Oh, on this day where great feasts and celebrations came into the gray walls of Policharki, this became my most cherished moment. This woman was so beautiful and brought me the happiest news of my life. In one clever sentence she had revealed only to me that both my brothers were being released. It was the first time in over two months that I finally heard something about my mother, about my family, and it was everything that I had wanted to hear. It was so hard keeping emotions deep down inside of you in prison, as a hard exterior was something you needed to gain respect as a man. Even though I wanted to dance, I couldn't – it would be childish. But the people inside my head were doing back flips. All the torture, all the lies, and living under the threat of exposure and death every day, had all been worth it. My two dear, sweet brothers were home with my mother. Even the Satan inside of me could not tear that away.

The following morning Dr. Shah again asked me to eat with him. Dagerwal was there too. We had a good breakfast, joked more openly than we could at the Khad with one another, talked, and played chess.

For the first two weeks it had been like a pajama party. The university student room was often full with vibrant energy, like an innocent little fraternity. Then, two weeks after I arrived in jail, all of the university and high-school kids that were arrested during the demonstration were taken to the court. They each pleaded guilty, said they were so sorry demonstrating against the revolutionary government, and asked for forgiveness. The government saw a perfect opportunity to use their confessions for propaganda and ran it on both the television and radio news. It was amazing that this was the story of how television came to Afghanistan, but truly, stories like these were the entire reason we joined the era of mass communications. All but three of the Kabul students were release.

The first not to be released was a medical student who was a couple years ahead of me - Shaker from Badakhshan. The second was a student from Kunduz, I believe his name was Wakil, a student of the Faculty of Economics in his fourth year. The third was a Hindu – Ashokomar, a fourth year science student. Each of them, instead of asking for forgiveness, had defended their actions in court, confronting the court about the Red Army's invasion and the killing of our innocent people. For this offense, Shaker and Wakil were sentenced to eight years in prison and Ashokomar was sentenced to one.

Politically Ashokomar was better educated and more active than Shaker or Wakil, but since he was Hindu, he was sentenced to far fewer years. Some of our roommates joked with him about his sentence: that since he was Hindu, no one wanted to take him seriously.

Ashokomar's first response, a fiery one, was to talk about taking a case of religious discrimination to court – if only he could. A hard turn of irony in a nation that hated Hindus so much that they could not bring themselves to believe that they were capable of patriotism.

They had lived in Afghanistan generation after generation, but we still believed they are simply visiting. We didn't believe they belonged in either our society or our nation. Ashokomar laughed at the joke with them, though he complained about it with a few of us. Ashokomar loved our country of Afghanistan as much as anybody in that room, and was willing to stand up firmer and taller than the majority of them. Still, of the three left behind, he was still left out in the cold. Even the communist judge, who did not even believe in Islam, did not take his patriotism seriously.

Once all the university kids had been released, the gigantic room turned from a frat party into a hollow cavern of boredom. More than anything, a cavern of silence. The room was larger than any we dared to imagine sleeping in before, but with the quiet it felt as cramped and tiny as a grave. I felt like those concrete walls were down around my neck. For the first time I really feel like I was in jail. It was several weeks before we adjusted to our new reality.

Without the constant socializing, I tried to make myself busier with the few books available to us. I asked my mother to bring a few of my poetry books, which others would soon begin to borrow from me, and the other roommates also had a few books we all shared. In the true spirit of "Communism", we formed a tiny community library. Books were as scarce and expensive as they were in Kabul. We could not afford to buy them most of the time, so some people even handwrote their own books to read. It was much cheaper that way. We were transcribing the works of others or writing our own pieces, as if Guttenberg had never been born.

Shaker, one of the boys who stood up to the court, was always doing that. Always he was busy writing. The second thing I was doing to make myself busy was writing myself, mostly defenses for the other inmates to take into the courts. When the communists sent the inmates to court, the only thing they received from the government was a small file but a couple of pages thick. The first part was a list of the accusations against them. Then, based on laws that belonged to the same regime they just toppled, which they were denouncing as mean and cruel laws in the public square, they charged the prisoners as if they had believed in it all their lives. The allegations were always exaggerated, replete with lies and total fabrications to fill in the gaps. At the end of it they would always ask the judge to punish us to the full extent of the law.

The judges themselves all communist judges, appointed by the communist government. In reality, the defense and what we said in court would mean nothing, but we did it anyways, because, as it is with human nature, when in trouble we want to hope for the best. I didn't take a penny in return. Most of my clients were simply asking me to beg the judge for their release. Their defense was filled with lies and fabrication, followed by asking for mercy at the tail end. In these courts of lies, whoever was able to spin the most beautiful thread usually came out ahead. Conviction trumped truth every time. Almost no one in that prison was in there for any reason other than their deep desire to see the slaughter of their neighbors come to an end.

The typical defense stated that the man was the family breadwinner (which was in most cases true), asked the judge to please forgive him, or stated that they were fooled by the rebels, but that now they regret their actions and want to have a chance to prove that they were good citizens. Or I stated on their behalf simply that there was insufficient evidence, and that my client had been wrongly accused. Or, one of my favorites, that the young man had been arrested by a jealous member of the communist party over a girl who had agreed to marry the accused.

Believe me, none of my clients deserved in any way to truly be called political prisoners. They were simple Afghans. The majority of those Afghans who had any real political views had been arrested in the first months after the coup and had been dead a long time. I myself was embarrassed to even call myself a "political prisoner", but I was one of the most active people on the outside of those now confined. 96% of our country was illiterate. Even those of us that did read did not know anything about politics.

We were not only illiterate, but so isolated that 90% of our Mullahs still believed that no one had gone to the moon yet, because the sky was guarded by angels and they would never allow such a thing to happen. The other 10% believed that the nonbelievers (Christians and Jews) had stolen the idea from the Quran. We only produced enough food to feed 50% of the people. It would seem a country ripe for Communism, but the Communism in Afghanistan was nothing more than an ideological shield for the establishing of yet another tyrannical dictatorship. True Communism was supposed to feed the people, not funnel the resources of the nation even more towards the rich. From what I could see though, that is exactly what was happening.

Even the communists themselves were confused as to what to call us, what to call to themselves, and what to call their so-called coup. According to the teachings of Communism I read while in prison, a revolution happens in an industrialized country with a labor class. The lower class stands against the capitalists with sticks and stones and topples the government, breaking any army or police force supporting the government. But in Afghanistan there was no industrial state, nor a class of laborers.

Industrialization had not come to Afghanistan, thus skipping a key era in Marx's progression towards Communism. Without industrialization and an industrialized working class, there could be no real revolution. They were calling it a revolution, but 99.99% of Afghans didn't even know what an electric screwdriver was, let alone a mass production factory, or any of the other basic components of a post-industrial society.

Yet, this confused communist government was arresting us by the thousands as enemies of figment classes, and calling us political prisoners. Although the literacy rate in the prison was at least ten times what it was outside those walls, still 80% of people in that jail could not even pronounce the word Communism. So, it was up to me and people like me, to act as an attorney, and to beg the judges to let our "clients" go. It was also why there were no politically unifying groups in Afghan prisons. The parties of the central square were not present here. There were just people, trying to get through the day, looking forward to getting a three line letter at the end of the week from somebody they knew on the outside… 50 % percent of us with family members that could write anyways. It always amazes me that in America there are so many prison gangs. In Afghanistan, those that would organize were killed before they could, and those that might organize knew that such actions meant death.

.Seven months after I had been arrested winter was in full swing. Only then did I finally receive my own court papers. I poured over them, looking at all the exaggerated allegations. They called me one of the most dangerous political leaders in Afghanistan. It made me quite curious, actually, as to how they came up with the majority of the anti-government activity they said I had done. I was charged with ten times what I was, and one hundred times more than what they had on me. As I began to write my own defense though, I found it far more difficult than I found writing defenses for my fellow inmates.

I rejected, I disputed, and I haggled with myself. All the while knowing that it made very little difference. The only thing I refused to do was beg for mercy. I would never beg to be released, and plead that I understood that all of my actions were wrong. I would also not play hero. What was said in court would never be heard by anyone, unless the Soviets deemed it "newsworthy", so playing it up would serve no purpose. Only two things would happen then: either I would be hanged, or sent back to interrogation. I was not a political leader. Political leaders negotiate treaties and pave roads. I was but a twenty-year-old university kid, and though imploring the judge for mercy might have helped, I knew I could not bring myself to do it. That would be spitting in the face of the blood soaked soils of Afghanistan, it would be like throwing to the dogs that blood soaked stick I had picked up while trying to usher my brothers home.

Three weeks later I was taken to court with fourteen other people. The Revolutionary court was in Shahr-e-naw, close to where I had been interrogated. We arrived there about ten in the morning. The judge was fast. Every ten to fifteen minutes he asked one of us to give our defense, and then another person was brought right afterwards. By noon, half of us were done, and the judge took a half hour break for lunch. There is no food for the accused, not that we expected any. It was 2pm when I entered the court. I said hello to the judge, who introduced himself as Kareem Shadan.

I knew this last name. His brother Abdullah Shadan was one of the best radio anchors in Afghanistan and a poetry critic. His brother's wife – Sema Shadan – was also in radio, and read classic Afghan poems on her late night show. The show was really popular in Kabul. They were both theater artists and had appeared in Afghan films. The nepotism in Afghanistan was really quite something in those days.

The judge asked for my defense and I handed it to him. My defense was a long one, about five pages. In court of illiterates, it was like a novel. As he read it, I quietly watched to tried to catch any changes in his energy or demeanor. But he read the pages in a stoic manner.

Once he had completed his review, he raised his head. "Very well written," he said.

He then began talking with me about my involvement in the Kabul University association. He discussed my writing skills, and then we went into classic poetry and the writers he liked. The judge was incredibly knowledgeable. As we talk I saw that he was beginning to like me. For a moment we both forgot what the purpose of my being there was. We traveled centuries into our Dari literature. While everyone else had only taken fifteen minutes, we spend three hours together. Finally, he thanked me for being there. From his eyes I felt like there was something in him that pushed him towards setting me free. I could not believe he had the power to do this, but still I hoped. The entire experience, from arrest to my day in court, appeared to be punctuated with intellectualism in the most bizarre places. It was as if even the strongest communist walls could not keep the drafts of truth from breaking through.

Afterwards I rejoined my compatriots as we waited for sentencing. They called the name of each person in our group and, one by one, they would come outside the room with the sentences. One year was the shortest sentence, fourteen years was the longest. Nobody calls my name. Already there had been three hours in the chambers of the judge that they waited through, now there was more. The blasé nature of the moment is stunning when I think back to it. Men, sentenced to spend years of their life behind bars, seemingly more upset about missing dinner than what the judge had handed down.

It was getting dark outside when suddenly I saw Munir. Munir was a classmate of mine from Kabul University. He was a high level communist, we all hated him. He had sent many people to die in the prisons during the reign of the Khalqis. Yet now, the snake suddenly acted as if he was pure Parchami. He was the head of the Medical Faculty's communist youth association.

Munir entered the judge's office. Then, a few minutes later, I saw my interrogator, my Lala. On the way into the judge's office he greeted me very kindly, coming right over to me. Half an hour later, Munir exited, followed by my Lala a few minutes after that. Again my Lala came over to me for a few moments to talk with me. He asked me how I was doing, and I said fine. He asked me about other inmates; I said that everybody was okay except for Alimohamad and his friend, who had been sick for long time. I asked him if he could release them for "I am afraid they will not make it for long". He said nothing, and then he said goodbye.

After another few minutes, they called me in. The judge handed me my paper.

"*Too Shafie ullah Walade Sayed Aulliah Nesbate jurmi ke Murtakeb shudy, bah panj sal habs mahkoom gardedy ta baese zajre khodet wa eberate degaran gardad.*" And with that, I was sentenced for five years behind bars. I shook the judge's hands and then I left.

It was about nine or nine-thirty when we arrived back at the jail. All our friends were waiting to see what had happened to us. All of mine are crowded together. As I enter, they embrace me. "Five years," I tell them... five years.

Among the crowed I saw Alimohamad and his friend, whose name I cannot recall. They hugged and kissed me too. "I saw our interrogator," I told them both.

"Oh yes?"

"Yes, and I told him about you guys. I told him that you guys were sick and I asked him if he could let you go." They were over-joyed, though we all knew that the chances of release were slim. It was no lie. They were both constantly ill, especially Alimohamad. Once he was so sick that he was not able to walk to the restroom. We had a doctor come once a week, but he had no medication on him except for painkillers. Though I am sure five hundred years ago, the last time people lived in such a place, such relief would have been a godsend. A week before, Fakhrodin, one of our roommates, had to put him on his shoulder take him to the third level, to the little room they called the "hospital". Fakhrodin got so rough with the jail physician over him that he ended up being severely punished. Here all good deeds were rewarded with punishment.

By ten o'clock at night, we were all sitting in the room when we heard a voice announce the names of Alimohamad and his friend. At that time of night the only reason they announced your name was for your execution. I rushed to the room's gate; they were both in the room across from us. A few minutes later I saw Alimohamad and his friend come to the door. A guard unlocked the door and they both came outside. They both had all their belongings in hand. One of the boys in my room asked the guard where they were going. "They are going home," He replied.

"God, that Lala has done exactly what I have asked him..." I whispered to myself. I could not believe my eyes. To this date whenever I remember, I tell myself that I need to find that Lala and thank him. A Parchami, a communist... look what a heart he had.

It was winter. In the summer we broke some of our room's glass windows, as the heat was unbearable, but now it was too cold. The building was made of concrete with no insulation. It was located in the middle of a desert in a wide valley, and the winter winds chilled us to the bone. We managed to cover the holes with plastic, but the plastic ended up blocking the fresh air from getting in. By this time the cell was no longer empty, and pack with more people than before. 140 people in an eighty by eighty foot room was just too much. Our breath, and sweat escaping from our pores, simply condensed on the concrete ceiling and began to rain down back upon us.

Actual showering in the winter was nightmarish. We didn't have a lot of water or a place to take showers more often than not to begin with. There was only one 15 by 15 foot room in the general washroom area, and we would be lucky to have a turn every two weeks. Then in the winter the room was so cold that we risked hypothermia washing ourselves. To keep warm, we had to go into the shower in groups of ten or so to avoid serious problems with the cold.

We first took an empty five gallon bucket filled it up with very slow flowing water. Then at the same time we took water from it with a smaller bucket in order to throw it over our heads and bodies. As soon as the freezing cold water touched our bodies, as if you threw water into the hot metal, a thick fog filled the room. We began shivering as if it we were entering the final moments of our lives. The cold water sucked out all of our body heat. As quickly as possible we soaped our bodies and then poured more of the water over us. As soon as we dried ourselves, we put our robes on and rushed to our room to wrap ourselves in our blankets. Often we would shiver for fifteen or twenty minutes more before our bodies warmed.

By the time my first year anniversary came, the jail was getting crowded. Slowly but surely, they stacked more and more of us in upon each other. The new Parcham government was able to keep many of its promises against the brutality of the Khalqi wing of the communist party, but the more people they crowd into the cells, the more we realized that things could change at a moment's notice.

As the jail became more crowded, they imposed more and more restrictions on us. They no longer allowed us to go outside for the whole day. They now let each floor out only on certain days, and, to be honest, we could not all fit in the yard now even if we wanted to. The thousands of us wandering the ground outside sent up an expression of dust into the air from every footstep, particles that combined into a choking cloud.

A year and a half after my arrest the jail was overflowing. They took away our ability to bring in books from the outside. Most of the time they no longer allowed our families to send any outside food. The money they sent had lost much of its use, as the little store was now almost always closed, and more often than not, empty. The food became worse. One day they stopped giving us breakfast, only providing lunch and dinner. For lunch we had an unwashed rice dish with lots of sand in it, which we were not able to chew and were just swallowing, and for dinner they provided a slosh of a soup with only one potato for ten people. Sometimes the soup was green pea, most of the time it was turnip. The soup was so watered down you couldn't taste much, if you'd wanted to taste it at all. It got to the point where almost every single day they only provided a turnip – cheaper than the potato. For a group of non-political prisoners, we began to formulate a hatred of turnip close to our hatred of the Soviets.

I remember one day when an inmate was saying goodbye to us, just before he was to be released. He told us, as those of us who were leaving often did, that if we had any messages for our families, to send them with him. Usually the only people who would speak up were those that needed something important. As he was about to leave, I shouted, "I have a message: please tell those stupid farmers to stop growing turnips."

As time went on, worms started getting into the soup. The green peas were infested with maggots, but they just cooked them and sent them to the prisoners anyways. Some people stopped eating. But by that point, I had learned to just eat whatever they sent you – worms and all. There was still a loaf of bread a day, but the larger prisoners soon began to starve because of the lack of food.

Since banning outside books, they soon opened a little library in the jail and filled it with the books of Lenin, Marx, Gorky, and a few Iranian communist writers. The number of books was maybe around one hundred. The hatred of the prisoners kept most of them from reading them, but I didn't mind. Day and night I began to read the books and learn them. There imprisoned by the communists I read all of Lenin's books, works on Dialectical Materialism, and economics books like Das Kapital. One of the inmates, Baqi Khan, who was like a self-taught professor, helped me a lot when he was housed with me for a few months.

Although the government was being blamed for anti-Islamic ideology, from what I could see the communists were quite open-minded. We could pray as much as we wanted, that never changed. Though while we were all in those rooms we didn't have the Azan from a loud speaker, each room had its own Muhazen (a person with a loud voice to do the Azan) and we sounded five times a day. Then, every few hours, we would all stand together and do a Jamaat (collective prayer).

By my second winter in prison, things were beginning to seem as if they would just start laying us one on top of the other. They continued to add inmates into the rooms without adding more toilets. The use of toilets had become one of our biggest concerns. There were very limited toilets on each floor. There used to be not even enough when we had 1000 people on each floor, but they had now packed in over 2500 people per floor, without expanding our options. They once had allowed us to use the toilet before bed, but now they often locked them away from us. The food was so rotten that many of the inmates began to develop serious stomach conditions, and of course, diarrhea.

Imagine a detainee, seventy years old and weak, with diarrhea that has to try and keep it in the whole night, until they allowed us to use the toilets in the morning. We were face to face with human waste on a daily basis and the line could be as long as four hours. This period of my life in prison was, to be honest, often spent largely in line for those ten toilets – waiting in line with the other 2500 roommates who relied on the same facility. A two hour wait was the minimum, on a very good day.

Adding to the problem: a lot of people in the jail had slowly been turned by the Pakistan led fundamentalist Muslim organizations. According to them, the use of toilet paper is a grave sin, as the holy Quran was written on paper. So, to them, paper was something holy, and they were not about to let others clean their asses with something holy! Instead, they used uncooked bricks: breaking them into little squares, rubbing themselves clean, and throwing the pieces in the toilet. The real problem was that there were no uncooked bricks available at Policharki, so when we went outside on our walking breaks, they just collect little pieces of stone from the yard to use. Stone after stone began to clog the toilets, until the toilets were shut down altogether and one of the few plumbers in Afghanistan was called in.

I remember, one day, about twenty of us were having a conversation. Someone asked us all what each person's best dream was. Out of the twenty of us, the vast majority's dream was to have unrestricted access to a toilet: to be able to go and sit for as long as they wanted without anyone disturbing them! It certainly was my dream

one day. I can write a book only about those toilet stories. To dis-
allow men from being able to relieve themselves, was something
you cannot even imagine, especially on such a grand scale.

During my third winter in Policharki, the jail was well over
capacity and they were continuously forcing more of us in together.
In each room built for fifty people, we had over three hundred. We
were allowed to go outside only once a week, only for a couple of
hours, and that was it.

There was one exceptionally cold morning that they gave us
our walking day. I was walking outside with a couple of my roommates, walking around the building as I had for many years now. We
would especially be on the lookout for newcomers with news of the
outside. As we were walking, we saw a whole new group of prisoners: about forty or fifty of them. Curious, we scoured their faces…
Among them we saw something that, even for my wildest dreams
was unusual. For a moment I thought that I was hallucinating. There
among them was this little kid, about five years old, at the most six.
It wasn't that we didn't have any juvenile prisoners before that, but
sending small children to jail was not something we had witnessed
before. The tiny little tip of his nose and his ears were red with the
cold. I knew at that moment, that this small child had no idea where
he was or why.

But instead of being upset, he was running everywhere. As far
as he was concerned, this was just another space to play. He looked
like a little panda cub at a zoo, rolling around without a care in the
world. It was beautiful. It had been many years since I had seen a
child at play. I was only 22 or 23, and yet I was already an old man.
We were motionless.

One of the guards always came out to watch over us. That day
it was Jora, an Uzbek guard from the north of Afghanistan. Jora
was not a communist and deep inside a very nice man, but he really
was stupid. He always had this belt hanging over his shoulder as a
warning for us, and when the time was over he had a habit of hitting us with it. So when our walking timer was over, Jora started
shouting, "Get back to your rooms, come on get back." But that
little boy was so innocent that he didn't understand—that he was a
guard and that we were prisoners—so the child ran up behind Jora

and began hanging off the belt. All the prisoners began to laugh hysterically. Jora ran after the kid, but could not catch the child for the life of him. A few minutes later, the kid ran up and hung off the belt again, sending Jora running about the yard.

Talking with some of my friends who were in the other rooms, we found out that little Panda was in the room just next to us. From that day forward, our yard time would be with Panda. It was such a pleasure to see him playing, even it was heartbreaking to look just up over his head to see where. Every once in a while he would take out a little toy harmonica, especially when our friend Ustad Sedeq would hold him. "You better play, or else I am going to hold onto you forever!" Ustad would say, and little Panda would see no option, and plays. We loved that.

The restrictions around this time started to lift a little bit. We were allowed once again to bring books into the jail from the outside. The little store we had was open more often and always well stocked. They gave us new bed sheets and some new blankets. Even the food quality had improved, and breakfast returned. The change was accompanied by several rumors. Some said it was because of the international pressure on the Afghan government to treat its prisoners in accordance with international law, some said the government was soon going to set us free and before doing so were treating us better to wash away our bad memories. All kinds of rumors were circulating, but finally they let us know what was really happening… Dr. Najibulah, the head of the communist secret service, was about to visit. But that in itself was nothing—he had visited a year before when conditions were horrible and nothing changed.

Soon they also told us that he was to be accompanied by guests who wanted to see the prison's conditions. His friend: a member of Indian communist party politburo. Everything in Policharki happened for a reason like this. The Soviets were obviously hoping that through the Indian communist party, everyone in the world would know that they were treating the Afghan political prisoners humanely. Everything finally made sense. We knew that it would do nothing for us, but we knew it would affect one little prisoner: Panda. Although Najibulah was truly famous for his brutality, Panda, with one sweet little smile, could cause everything to come crashing down around him. So the little kid's roommates began coaching him. Afghan kids were usually shy, but not little Panda. The roommates told him, as Najibulah came in, to just run, hold him tight, and ask him to release you. To say, "I am innocent, just let me go."

A few weeks later, they locked us all in. They were not even allowing us to go to the restrooms until he left the building. They told us that only those who needed it the most could go, and only one by one! Can you believe that? They told twenty thousand inmates, half of which had diarrhea, not to use the restrooms unless they really needed it! It is a joke brother, you need to laugh! We each received a warning to be nice to the visitors. No provocative questions were allowed.

In the morning we received a better breakfast than usual. They even distributed some pencils and some paper for us, to convince this Indian guy that we even had the freedom to express ourselves. Around 11am the guards began telling everybody on our floor (the third floor), block two, that Dr. Najibulah had arrived on our floor. There was a total silence, we were not even breathing aloud. All we could hear were the footsteps of the devil approaching us, Najibulah and his companions. The hall was a long and narrow one with concrete walls and floor. You could clearly hear anyone walking there, especially when there was silence.

We next hear the guard opening our door's lock, and a bunch of people enter. Najibulah is very noticeable. He is overweight, tall, with a puffy face. His Indian guest is walking along side him. He is a tall, dark, but slim guy. He walks around the room and greets us, then talks a little and promises that, soon, when the situation improved, we would be released! You could tell every person in the room had to keep themselves from simply laughing out loud, but a terrible fear kept us still and quiet. Once he left our room, they walk into the next one. Panda is a 100 % ready. His roommates have already convinced the guard at the door to allow little Panda to go out and talk with Najibulah. They convinced the guard that Najibulah was such a nice guy he probably did not even know about this child and that, once he saw him, he would take him with him and release him.

The guard, another non-communist, agreed. He, just as everybody in the entire prison, did not see any reason for a little kid to be in there. Since nobody knew for sure whether Najibulah was going to go to every room or not, and nobody wanted Panda to miss his chance to see his "angel", the guard agreed that as soon as Najibulah was close to the gate of the room that he would let little Panda outside into the hall to see him.

So, courageous little Panda ran outside. Running right towards him, he grabbed the thigh of Najibulah and begged him to let him go.

Najibulah, embarrassed in front of his Indian friend, shook his thigh as hard as he could. Little Panda hit the concrete wall, bounced back, and the frightened guard was so terrified that he simply threw him back into the room. Everybody stopped moving. The guard covered his actions by pretending that he didn't see him, and had nothing to do with it. He could have been hanged, I don't blame him. Little Panda was in that jail for at least another month.

After more than three years in prison, the officials had come to mark me as one of the most dangerous prisoners. Dangerous in there, however, did not mean that I posed a threat to other prisoners or prison personnel. It only meant that I had not been as quiet as the others. I continued to stand up against the jail personnel for my rights as a prisoner and my other brothers' rights, like few other prisoners did. They would also see me reading books, and helping others when they had a question. In this jail, when they saw someone was busy reading, they automatically labeled them a threat.

Unlike in the beginning, we had hundreds of spies in the jail now. The majority were just prisoners openly spying for the government with the hope that they would be able to use the bathroom more regularly, or be able to steal a few more spoonfuls of soup from other prisoner's rations, or maybe even receive a reduced sentence, although days in the prison were so harsh that a distant point in the future was something they could not always afford to keep in their minds.

The spies have nothing much to report however. We were not sophisticated politicians or criminals who would plan a break from jail, or send orders to the outside to topple the government. So though the news they conveyed was trivial, it carried an awkward air of importance: things like you having a better relationship with others for a few weeks. Once you were marked by the jail security personnel, they would begin to move you around from room to room. Due to these kinds of repeated reports and a few arguments I had with the guards, they believed that I was inciting the other prisoners against the system. To prevent me from doing any such thing, they just kept moving me from room to room. They did not want me to be in a room long enough to associate with other prisoners. About every week they read my name and told me to take my belongings with me: a few pairs of clothing, a few books if the restrictions were looser that week, and a few cans of food.

Even the security personnel knew me as Doctor Shafie now. When they read my name, they always read it as "Dr. Shafie". I always gave them hard time, when they read my name I didn't answer at first, and let them go around for a while. Finally the room spies would go outside and tell them about me. Then they'd come back, upset, and ask me why I didn't respond. I'd say, "You did not read my name. I am not a doctor, and you guys were looking for Dr. Shafie."

I would then export my things in a small iron box. The process satisfied them that they were preventing something big from happening. In the beginning it had the effect of isolating me, but after a while I had been in every room in the prison enough times that I knew a lot of people in every one of the blocks. I began to learn not to waste any time when I entered a new room: I quickly became a friend to everybody I met, and started associating with all of them.

This enabled me to get a lot of information and learn a lot about the inside of the jail, even about what was going on outside the jail, within every corner of the country. Everywhere they took me I met new prisoners, belonging to all kinds of political organizations... as over time the non-political nature of the body of prisoners was slowly changing. They were, in a very clear sense, creating radicals where there had been none before. I met all kinds of people from all over Afghanistan, which enabled me to know about all different kinds of customs, cultures, languages, and different religious beliefs, though those, of course, were all within the frame of Islam.

It really transformed me. During this time I came to meet some of the best and some of the worst people in Afghanistan. Afghanistan had been on the route through for many of the world's great conquerors, and they always left a trace of their ethnicity behind. Some of the conquering armies just stayed in Afghanistan, marrying local girls, and centuries of time had boiled us together, as one nation.

Together we were knotted like Afghani rugs by one beautiful language: Dari. Somehow, conquerors came to Afghanistan, invaded this country, slaughtered a lot of people, but then almost always adopted the Dari language as their own. Wherever they went, they took this language as a trophy with them, and the language spread all over the region, from India to Turkey and beyond. This was the language of the greatest philosophers, poets, and writers in southern Asia – all touched by the magical ripples of Dari through the ages. The language produced the most important scholars, philosophers, linguists, poets, writers, medical innovators, scientists, and much more. Some of the most important people, which Iran proudly claim as Iranians today, in fact belonged to today's Afghanistan, Tajikistan, and Uzbekistan. While Farsi, the Iranian language, stayed pretty much inside the territory of today's Iran, Dari (the sister language) developed and traveled all the way to the southern tip of India, to the borders of China, to Tajikistan, Uzbekistan, to Pakistan, to Azerbaijan, to Kirghizstan, to Turkmenistan, to Turkey, and beyond.

Until two centuries ago, the official language of the Indian people was Dari. It was the British occupation of India that changed that. Even today, the Indian language of Urdu, which is widely spoken in India, and is the language of all Indian movies, is a heavy mix of the Dari and Hindi languages. If someone speaks Urdu, we can always understand a lot of it, including the songs. If you visit the Taj Mahal and other historic sites around India, you will see lots of beautiful poetry being carved into the walls of the buildings. All are in the Dari language, a language that has done a lot for the people of this whole region.

Although we have many different races, and smaller local languages and a variety of Islamic religious practices, the Afghan people are the most simple, kind, polite, brave (too brave in many cases), extremely hospitable, honest, and friendly people that I have ever met then or since. A very poor person in Afghanistan will share their only bite of food with you. The poorer they are the purer they are.

Though language bound me close to the more beautiful souls trapped inside that concrete block, I met some of the worst criminals in there as well. For months, I was a roommate of Faqeer Muhammad Faqeer, the Interior Minister for Hafizullah Amin, and Professor Soma, Amin's High Education Minister. I met Shah Wali-Wali, the Prime Minister for Hafizullah Amin, and many more of his administration and Ministers.

These were the people who were responsible for killing of tens of thousands of Afghans. Faqeer Muhammad Faqeer was Hafizullah Amin's number one man, and a pure ideologue. One day I asked him that as the KGB and Parchamis were alleging that Hafizullah Amin was an agent of the CIA, and he had known him for years and years, what he thought about it? He said that he knew, like daylight, that Hafizullah Amin was a pure communist, but since the Khalqis were a firm believer in the Soviets, if the KGB said Hafizullah Amin was a CIA agent, then Faqeer Mohamad Faqeer and his Khalqis fully agreed! Yet those high ranking communists, who were the head of the government for the first two years after the communist coup, were being jailed by their rival Parchamis, who now had the support of the KGB instead. One wondered if he would have labeled himself a CIA agent if they told him to.

The more wonderful people in that prison more than balanced out the evil men I was housed with every so often. It was in this jail that I met Khal Muhammad, an inmate from Panjsher. I called him Kaka, or uncle, because he was older than me and it is a great term of respect in Afghanistan. In his late forties, he had learned to read and write in jail. He went as high as the college level in Dari literature. He read some of the most complicated political books available to us in the jail.

But that is not what I remember him for. He never had a Paywaz. He was so poor that whenever my Paywaz sent me some food, if he was around I would call him to have lunch or dinner with me. Sometimes I shared some of my money with him, but he was always giving that money to the more needy ones. He was among the few inmates who were taking care of all the garbage on our floor, and was working at least ten hours a day. In return the inmates each gave him a half rupee a week. Now that totaled like a thousand rupees a month, which was not bad.

But he was not spending a rupee on himself. He was spending it on the poor and the needy. But that is also not why I truly remember him. I remember him because he was spending all that money in a secret manner on the people, so that no one would know. He did not want anybody to know what he did. Once, after a few years, someone from his family finally visited him in the jail. His family was not able enough to give him a lot, so they just brought him a new robe. We never saw that new robe on him. He only had those old torn up jail clothes. I became curious and started asking other inmates what happened to his new robe, and why he wasn't putting it on? I finally found out that he had given that away too, to one of the new inmates in need of a robe. Khal Muhammad was finally released after many years being behind bars, but lost his life in a military plane crash not many more years after that.

It was also in this jail that I met Allahmohamad. Allahmohamad was a young guy, perhaps 22 years old. Allahmohamad was arrested with an Afghan legendary hero—Majid Kalakani. When I was first brought to Khad, across from the room I was being interrogated there was a two story building. A Russian military tank was parked in front of the entry door, aimed directly at it. The two story building was completely surrounded at all times with dozens of young Soviet soldiers – all there to guard Majid. Not even Afghan secret service members were allowed to enter that building, as Majid was extremely popular and the KGB had fear that even the Afghan secret service agents might help him escape.

Majid was the first anti-Soviet Afghan who was executed by the Parcham and the KGB after the Soviet invasion. When I was in Khad, it happened during my first month of interrogations that I heard the news from a radio mounted on the top of the building wall for the prisoners. That was a very sad day for all of us in the detention center. A couple of weeks after that, I was in the room with Dr. Shah, when one day the guards transferred three new inmates to our building. Two were still able to walk by themselves, in shackles, the other was so weak that he was unable to, and was on the shoulder of quite a big guard. They were put into the very last room, the opposite end of the row from us. They were not even allowed to go out to walk in the yard. Only a couple of days a week were they brought outside for a walk, always with three guards accompanying them. We were all curious as to who they were. At the time I did not know Allahmohamad, but over a year later I was introduced to him in block number one of Policharki, where he was detained.

Block number one was a totally different facility. It had three levels of small rooms. Perhaps twelve by fifteen feet. The rooms had one bathroom inside of them (no waiting in line) and were designed for four people, but they put about twelve to fifteen of us in there. The facility was usually for the inmates with more serious charges. The majority of the inmates in this block were facing the death penalty. A lot of people I met in that facility were executed, one by one, over time. I was brought in there for first time at the beginning of my second year, due to some arguments with the guards where I was beaten badly and, in addition, sent to a more restricted facility as punishment.

It was on block one that I became Allahmohamad's roommate, and we soon became close friends. Allahmohamad, was interrogated for longer than any other prisoner I had ever heard of. He was tortured for months, and even now once every few months he was sent back to the Khad for additional interrogations, which always included torture. He was as hard as steel, and had not even told them his real name. His real name was Allahmohamad, and with us he always introduced himself as Allahmohamad, but with the interrogators and the jail personnel he never even responded when they called that name. He insisted that his name was Aziz, and that he was not from Shamaly, but from Kandahar.

They already knew him, he was well known. His older brother was one of the famous anti-government commanders, but Allahmohamad denied everything. He just insisted that he was Aziz from Kandahar. In no way did this help him, but it could not hurt him either. Nothing could, as he was to be executed, and what more could they do to him than that? What I will always remember about him was that he always woke very early in the morning to work out in the room. He never missed his work-out. At least an hour a day he would work out right there in the jail cell. Working out was not common in Afghanistan, especially in that jail.

I can tell you that he was probably the only one who was doing that in the entire twenty thousand prisoner population on a regular basis. And when he did his work-out, he was always trying to convince us to do the same thing. "You guys need to work out, because when this country is free again and we go outside, there will be lots of work for us to do. Our bodies need to function perfectly. A lot of damage has been done to this country, and we will need to work hard to do all the repairs." I will remember Allahmohamad for that until the day I die. Nothing could save him, but the hope in him shone brighter than in any other I have ever witnessed before or since.

He knew he was going to be executed without a shadow of a doubt unless a miracle happened, but never thought about that. He was only thinking about the day that we would kick the Russians out and break the chains of slavery from the hands and feet of our people. He always reminded us that this would be day one of the process, not the final day as so many might expect.

It was on block one that I met seven groups of prisoners, each containing of at least four or five or even more people, who were all alleged to have killed a sloppy communist singer named Khan Qarabaqhi. The groups were all related to different Islamic organizations. They were tortured so badly each of the seven groups confessed to the killing. Seven different groups, never having met each other before, belonging to different organizations, all confessed to the killing of the same man. And they were all sitting in that jail, convicted of one single crime they couldn't possibly have all committed, awaiting their execution.

It was also on block one that I met Najibulah. Najibulah's brother was an important member of Hezbi Islami Hekmatyar. In fact, he was in charge of the whole city of Kabul. When he was captured, a list of five thousand Hezbi Islami members was found at his house. They were all in code, but he himself broke the code for the secret service, under a false promise of release, and at least two thousand of their members, all from Kabul, were arrested.

After he was executed, they took his brother Najibulah and a bunch of their other high level members for execution. While they were executing them though, a call was made by the secret service to the executioners that they needed Najibulah still, because they had arrested some new members of their organization and needed Najibulah's information about them. It was only a few seconds before his execution, and they untied him to be brought back for more torture.

He had already witnessed the others executions, and was so shocked that he lost his ability to speak. Something messed up inside his brain and he was never able to talk again. They were always giving him pen and paper to write what he wanted to say. They promised him that if he cooperated again, they would forgive him this time and not execute him. He did, he cooperated fully, once again, and sure enough, they executed him a few months later. It was in this block that I met people whose executions were announced on television as they sat right there beside us, watching the news themselves. We all heard together that they had already been executed, but there they are, just sitting next to us. You can imagine how that person feels—they are dead already as far as the state is concerned. There is no more hope. He knows that at any moment they will come to take him. Normally the man would just stand up, give us all a hug, go in the room, and as it is common with Muslims, do his last prayer. And, before he is even done, they come in, read his name, tie his hands, cover his eyes, and take him to be killed.

But although prison was tough, so far these had been the best years of my life. I was so lucky to be with so many excellent people. I was so lucky that God had given me a deep sense of humor; that I could always make things funny, laugh, and make others laugh along with me. One day in block number one, in one of those little rooms, we made so many jokes, and we were laughing so much, that finally a couple of guards opened our little door and screamed at us as loud as they could, "What are you stupid people laughing for, don't you know that you will soon be sent for execution?!?" In this room I was roommate with a best friend, Ustad Hamid, a Science Faculty teacher, living and teaching in East Coast now.

We stopped laughing. But as soon as they left we started laughing even louder than before. For many life in this prison was so ugly, so hard, so boring, that they would simply pray for God to take them into a deep sleep for as many years as they were incarcerated, and wake them only on the day of their release. But my prayers were very different. Often I would pray, "God, please make these days go a little slower. I don't even feel how they are passing."

As year four passed by, it had been almost one year since I had been sent to blocks two, three, or four, where the majority of the prisoners were kept. For over a year I had been moved around block one, through the smallest rooms they had. Almost every person I had met when I first came into the block was now dead. For over a year I watching dozens of men live out their last days, and then be whisked away to a heartless execution with a bag over their head or fold over their eyes—robbing them of their last few visions in life.

My dear friend Allahmohamad was gone. He had been executed almost one and a half years ago at this point. He was so full of life, so many were, but none like him. I imagined they would have needed an army to yank the life from his breast. Whenever our walking day came up and we were on different floors, he would always pull himself up, holding onto the iron bars on the room's little window, to wave to us as they left him inside. He knew we were so worried about him; he wanted to let us know that he was still alive.

I'll never forget the last day I saw him. It was the day before he was sent to die. Around 4pm we were walking outside and he pulled himself up to the little window as usual, waving . The image was burned into my mind. Just at the tail end of its stay in my short term memory, word of his execution came, and the memory lit fire. It seared its way into the most enduring part of me.

In this jail, nobody wanted to be seen crying. You needed to be tough, a tough Afghani man. I never even shed tears when I heard Allahmohamad was executed. But for many years, even after I was released, I was dreaming of him. I was talking with him. I dreamt that I would tell him about how sad we all were when we heard of his death. In that dream, I cried. Many times I would wake up, and my pillow would be wet, soaking wet, and tears were still flowing from my eyes. I dearly loved Allahmohamad.

Before he died he had offered me his watch. "Shafie," he said, "I want you to take my watch, to remember me. I have heard that when they execute the prisoners, they steal all their belongings. I don't want them to have my watch; I want a friend to have it." I always regret that I refused it. I did not want to accept that; it would have been like admitting that he would be executed one day. He would always ask me, I always tell him no,no one will execute you, but one time I finally told him, "Allahmohamad, if they take you from us, let them take your watch too. If I can, one day, I will take both back from them." The spirit of those brazen words is now faded for me, and I wish that I had simply taken the watch.

I must have met over twenty thousand people in my first three years there, though for the last year I had been completely isolated. I learned a lot being with all these people. Even now, in isolation, I was still always meeting new prisoners, much less in number than before, but each of them were of a much higher caliber. They were more knowledgeable, and more involved.

When I was brought in Policharki four years prior, there were not many prisoners there yet. In fact, we were among the first prisoners of that new regime—the first prisoners to be taken since the Soviet occupation. Four years later there were over thirty thousand prisoners in the different blocks of that jail. In the beginning, we all slept on the floor, but within one and half years the Jail had been turned into a plant for manufacturing "justice", and thousands of iron bunk beds were made for the prisoners, by the prisoners, in the prison itself, for use in the cells. It doubled the capacity of the jail, which helped for a while, but soon the jail became too full, even for the double beds.

We then were told that we had to put two of the double beds together and sleep three people on each level. That increased the capacity of the jail another 50%. That helped for a few months too, but soon the jail was overloaded again. Of course, they still did not build a single new toilet to go with the increased "bed space". And even eating the food became difficult, because we knew it would simply lead to another three hour wait in the line to the bathroom.

In that first year, we were all like brothers – united both socially and politically. We each shared the same goal, to free our country. We all opposed the Soviet invasion of our motherland. But soon enough we were all divided. When the war against Soviets started in Afghanistan, we did not care about outside world. We did not care who was supporting us or who was not. We did not care if Iran or Pakistan was leaving their borders open for us to seek shelter. In fact, running to Pakistan or Iran, or anywhere, was a cowardly and unmanly thing to do. We did not care if America was sending us money and weapons, or the Saudis, or the Chinese, or the Europeans, or not.

We had decided something then: we were determined to expel the Soviets from our country. That was the common goal, gluing us together like one strong, single body. Corruption entered the prison, and dependence began to reign as international attention began to rise. When the Soviets invaded our country, Iran did not care much, as they were busy fighting the Americans. When Khomeini was calling America the Big Satan, it was of help to the Soviets. It covered up a far more important issue, their focusing on American corporate endeavors—it covered up the fact that the Soviets were out to steal everything.

Pakistan was totally different than Iran. Our entire nation believed that half of Pakistan was Afghan land cut from Afghanistan as a result of the 1893 Duran Line treaty. It was designed by British colonial powers, during "Great Games" era, to be used as a buffer against the Russians. In 1947, when Pakistan was separated from India, they kept the Afghan land and refused to even discuss it. War between Afghanistan and Pakistan was always a prospect.

The Pakistanis were worried to death when they saw the Russians at their door step. They knew the Soviets were eyeing an expansion of their empire to the coast of the Indian Ocean. Helping the Afghan resistance was very important to Pakistani national security. At first... things soon changed though. The Afghan people's heroic resistance and their sacrifices in the face of the Soviet invasion of their motherland soon got the attention and the sympathy of hundreds of millions of people around the world. Soon, hundreds of millions of dollars were poured into Pakistan to help the Afghan movement. The temptation was strong. Many Pakistanis completely forgot about the Soviets, about the Afghan war, and about the dangers of a Soviet invasion of Pakistan. Looting took the place of concern, as corruption took the place of reason.

Pakistani officials soon became professional thieves. To sustain their looting, the first thing Pakistani Government did was try to convince as many donor countries as possible that it was too dangerous to submit money and aid directly to the grassroots in Afghanistan — the only method of donating ever shown to have worked in the history of mankind, and they disputed its efficacy! They managed to have direct aid pretty much banned. The Pakistani government then assembled a kind of shadow cabinet in Pakistan made up of Afghans that had fled the country and would remain loyal to Pakistan. This was easy. Hundreds of Ikhwanis (Muslim extremists), cowardly Afghans who left Afghanistan within days of the communist coup, were now living in Pakistan. They were just wandering around, jobless and homeless. Pakistan quickly put them together and began to call them "leaders".

But that was not enough. The Pakistanis knew that the Afghan people were a very proud people and, especially because of the land dispute they had with Pakistan, that the Afghans were always suspicious of Pakistan's intentions. They knew that the Afghans would not allow Pakistan to steal hundreds of millions of their aid money for long. They also knew that Afghans would in no way allow Pakistan to handpick their leaders outside of their borders. So the third thing Pakistan did… was to convert the way the Afghan-Soviet war was perceived from a freedom movement to a Jihad.

At that time, in Afghanistan, we were calling ourselves freedom fighters, not Mujahideen, and this prevented Pakistan from controlling the war in Afghanistan, as for as Afghans who were fighting against outsiders, Pakistan was an outsider too. They knew that this was a sensitive issue, and that Pakistan's interference would be interpreted as an invasion. Not necessarily an invasion of our country, but an invasion of our affairs and an invasion of our freedom. That was why they needed to take the word "freedom" out and replace it with the word Jihad, in order to turn Pakistanis from outsiders to insiders.

Jihad is a holy war in which Muslims fight against non-Muslims, and in Jihad not only are all Muslims the same, but it is their common duty, no matter where the Jihad is happening, to join the rank and file. Pakistan not only gained the "right" to become part of our war, but they gained the "right" to lead us. Because in Jihad, it is not important which country you belong to, it is only your qualifications that put you in charge as a leader. And resources, money, access— these were the qualifications Afghans did not have. Freedom was something we loved since I was a little boy in Afghanistan, but it was a word that foreign invaders on all sides was trying to transform into something less holy; into something satanic. Soon you could be marked as an infidel and a non-Muslim for calling yourself a freedom fighter, because Muslims in Jihad did not fight for land, or even freedom. Freedom belonged to "this life"; for a Muslim "this life" is not important, nor is the freedom of this life. Whoever called himself a freedom fighter became an infidel, an enemy of Islam, because he created a division among the Muslims.

Once the Pakistanis created their puppet Mujahideen leaders and set their manifesto of war before them, they did one more thing. They divided these Mujahideen into seven different groups, not friendly groups, but rivals. They claimed that they were each fighting for Islam, but that they were also thirsty for each others' blood. Not the leaders themselves, who were not killing each other because Pakistan needed them, but down below, in the lower ranks.

The ISI printed tens of thousands of membership cards and gave them all to their puppet Mujahideen leaders. Soon they were smuggled to villages all over Afghanistan. When these membership cards were delivered in Afghanistan, Afghans were unaware of the consequences. They all rushed, joined, and took membership cards as if they were gaining deeds to the ownership of some of the best land in the nation. Some received Gulbudin Hekmatyr's membership cards, some received Burhanudeen Rabani's cards, some Mawlawi Khalis's cards, some Sebghatullah Mujadidi's, some Gillani's, some Mawlawi Muhammad Nabi's, and soon they found themselves belonging to warring factions. The more I learned about what was going on outside, the more I realized how sinister a manipulation had befallen my dear country. We were being pitted against each other at every turn—manufactured outrage leading to death.

In order to control more territories, they started to fight each other. The situation turned extremely chaotic very fast. Soon other smaller branches and divisions were created among the members of the same groups. Heavier fighting broke out. Within a few years our country became a totally different war zone. Almost everybody received a machinegun, which they soon turned against both the invaders and their neighbors. Sometimes the fighting among these Mujahideen was so severe that it lasted for days on end Hundreds could be killed.

Over time more and more incoming inmates were members of the Mujahideen. They told me stories about how when two warring factions would begin to run out of ammunition, Soviet helicopters would show up and drop new cases of ammunition for both sides so that they could keep killing each other. Since a majority of the Mujahideen card holders and their commanders were uneducated, in order to justify their high-ranking positions they began to blame the invasion on the educated people of Afghanistan as much as they did on the Soviets.

They argued that if it was not for all our schools and universities, our kids would not have become communists and we would not have the Soviets in Afghanistan. For them it was the fault of the schools, of education, and of educated people. So, like the communists before them, they too now targeted all educated people, and began to burn the schools. First the word freedom became satanic, now the word education was just as evil. Anyone who had been educated started to learn that to survive in Afghanistan they needed to let their beard grow, put on a turban like the villagers, and never talk or raise suspicion about anything said around them. This is exactly what Pakistan and their puppets wanted. They wanted all the educated Afghans out, so they could not pose a threat to the Pakistani puppets, creating their own leadership in Afghanistan, and pushing Pakistan out.

While the high-ranking Mujahideen leaders were getting a lot of money from the ISI, the lower ranking members were securing their source of income from looting the Afghan people. Along all the main highways, the commanders put temporary posts to stop all the buses and were looting every passenger of whatever they had. Nobody could say a word, because they would be shot right there on the spot. They were taking hundreds of semis full of merchandize, confiscating the merchandise, and selling the trucks in Pakistan.

144

Sometimes they took people hostage and demanded a ransom from their families. Taking young boys and girls as sex slaves was also common among these "holy warriors".

In the villages too nothing was safe. If a commander or even a lower ranking Mujahid wanted to marry a girl, they could force their families into it. In Islam a Muslim is not allowed to marry a married woman, except if the husband was a non-Muslim, or an infidel Muslim. In many cases they wrongfully accused an innocent man, just to marry his beautiful wife.

Since the Mujahideen were so corrupt, and so much rivalry existed among the different groups, the Afghan intelligence service could easily infiltrate them, in order to use them even more effectively against each other. Sometimes the rival groups were spying for the Soviets directly, voluntarily, and telling them the hideouts of their rivals, allowing the Soviets to target them. Policharki became an exact reflection of this. The jail was now filled with spies and men looking to slit each other's throat. These were the men that Charlie Wilson bragged of, as pictures of the best mankind could offer. This, the war many are so proud of, they call it Charlie Wilson's War!

One might think that under these circumstances the communists would be winning, but the Mujahideen was not collapsing in any way. Because soon the ISI had infiltrated inside both factions of the communist party as well. Yes, Pakistan was now in charge of everything in Afghanistan that the Soviets weren't. I am not sure if CIA and American officials at this time didn't care or didn't know, but we all knew on block one of Policharki—these men on block one were, after all, the people who were meeting with the ISI and KGB every day. These were the men who took their money and executed their plans... only to be tossed aside like pawns in a game of chess between Pakistan and the Soviet Union. Afghanistan became the board for a more than deadly game.

The hatred of the United States among Mujahideen grew over time, despite the fact that their very existence was predicated upon American assistance. The ISI spent time grilling anti-Americanism into their agents, in order to ensure the United States could not enter the fray as well and just absorb what was left of Afghanistan from the Pakistanis during the years and after the war. The second thing came from the influx of anti-Semitic Arabs into the ranks who deplored the US support of Israel. This also was encouraged by ISI, because it was keeping the Americans from having direct relationship with Mujahideen.

I remember friends who were members of these groups telling me that they had orders to blow up bridges, buildings, and any other structure which was being built with American aid money—orders handed down from the groups soaking up the majority of that aid for themselves. The Americans always insisted on ensuring their name was inscribed on all things built with their money, in an effort to show Afghans that they were helping them. At the end of the day, they were simply marking their own works for demolition. They were also told to hunt down any Americans or American journalists they could find in the country, and to execute them.

Both the Islamic rebellion and the communists were rotting from the inside. For the ISI, it was like winning the biggest jackpot ever. International aid was reaching billions of dollars a year, and the Pakistanis were stealing eighty to ninety percent of it according to the men I knew who were involved in the theft, with the other ten percent largely going to send Jihad fighters in the shut Afghan mouths up. The last thing Pakistan wanted was for the war to end, and for all that money to dry up.

If the Mujahideen got stronger and the communist regime was on the verge of collapse, they would call the Mujahideen fighters back to their caves or make them busy fighting each other. And if the Red Army and the Afghan army posed a crucial threat to the existence of the Mujahideen, the ISI would send out all of the Mujahideen from their hideouts to fight the Soviets. This way they could make sure the war never ended, and keep the billions flowing. In other words, they were **recycling** the war in Afghanistan over and over again.

In the spring of 1984 I was still in block number one. In that block we had a television in the hall. Each night at about 8 pm they opened the doors for each floor, and we each went out in the hall to watch the news. They thought that if we saw the news and heard the government's propaganda it would help transform us into "good" Afghans, and it could curb our zeal. Watching the news was, in fact, mandatory. But we enjoyed it, just to go into the hall for half an hour and be with more inmates was entertaining. I can't remember exactly what I was doing, but I'm sure we were talking about something. Then, all of the sudden, an announcement came in over the news.

"The Afghanistan government is announcing that they will be releasing all prisoners that have served at least half their time."

I was sentenced for five years and had already served over four.

Within a week the Khad sent a couple dozen agents to make a list of all the prisoners who are eligible for release. During my Paywaze, my mother was ecstatic, and wrote me a very excited letter about the announcement. Three years had passed since all of my brothers and sisters had left Afghanistan. Each of them had been taken as refugees to the United States, including my youngest brother, who was a third or fourth grader when he had to escape. My mother was living alone, by herself. The only happiness she had was that every Friday she could come to the prison to get a short letter from me to ensure that I was alive and well. She stayed three years by herself alone waiting for me to be released. She was not going to leave me behind. Not only would my release mean that I would be free again, it meant that the entire family would be reunited from the far reaches of the globe for the first time in many years.

A couple months went by, and then one day, dozens of buses arrived inside the walls, all accompanied by Khad agents and their military back up. It was a busy day in Policharki. In each block they read the names of those eligible, then told them to pack and leave. A few thousand people were released that day. I waited all day to hear my name, but it never came. Soon I learned that I was not the only one, and that there were some other prisoners that had not been released too. My mother was heartbroken again, but hope was now alive. It was another two or three months before the Khad returned with more buses.

It was now almost four and half years since I had entered Policharki. In the early morning in block number one, one of my roommates, for some reason, was called to go to the office of the block. Upon his return back, there was a very different look about his face. "Mr. Doctor," he said... "I heard them call your name! I think you are on the new list of people to be released!"

For one last time I hid my emotions. When I heard the news, I barely smiled. Soon I heard them calling my name on our floor, and everybody got excited. For years I had been living with the walking dead, with men facing their very last days on earth. Today a name was called for a very different reason. All of them stood and embraced me excitedly. I told them "No, they may be just taking me to a different room."

But there is no way of convincing them otherwise, "God willing, you are going to be released."

As soon as the guard came to my door, he read my name, asked me to pack, and told me my release was going to be today. I still did not want to believe them. I opened my sheet metal box, took all of my medications, my can of food, some of my clothes and towels out "If I am being released, I want you guys to share my stuff. And if they take me to another room, then I will ask the officer to send someone to bring my things over."

I take my empty sheet metal box and kissed all of my roommates goodbye. While being abducted from my home in front of my family was the most shocking goodbye of my life, this was most definitely the most difficult. No other goodbye would ever be as hard once I left that prison. Hugging a man and knowing they are taking him off to die, and that you can do nothing... just watching someone take your friend, a person who was fighting for the same thing as you, to be executed, is something you cannot express in words.

The day I left prison was not a great day, but a sad one. I was leaving thousands of people behind me in that jail, and I had no idea what would happen to any of them. They would not be okay. I was happy, excited, but sad. One eye laughed, one eye cried, or the lips were smiling and the heart was bleeding. As I walked outside I saw about another hundred or so prisoners all being brought from other blocks. The main office for the jail was in the block number one, so they were rounding them all up there.

Once outside they read our names again, matching all our descriptions to make sure we were the right people. They then took us all to a designated area where they had a microphone. A few moments later, a high ranking official from the Khad took the microphone and began giving us a long lecture about the "democratic"

148

government, its goals, its projects, and told us all to help build a better Afghanistan. He then told us to move to a different place for a final check up and wait for the buses to take us to downtown Kabul.

While we are standing in the line, I saw a bunch of jail officials from block two coming to block number one. Among them I see a communist guard. I had not seen him since the day he sent me to the isolation of block one to rot over a year ago. I cannot recall his name, but remember him as Serbaz: the name those cowards were always calling themselves. Serbaz was the only reason I was detained in isolation, in those little cells for over a year in block one.

At the time I was housed in block two on the third floor, we had close to 300 people in that room. In the jail, whenever a communist guard was coming into our rooms for a check-up, we would try not to talk with each other, and hide the chess boards if we had any, along with any books or paper or pencils if we had them. In that particular room there was a Parchami member of the communist party imprisoned with us: I don't know if he was spying for the ISI or if he was arrested on some big theft charges, or what. But now in prison a lot of the Parchami guards and administrations knew him from the outside and gave him some privileges.

He could, for example, have his chess board and play chess without any restrictions. And he was a damn good chess player. I had just gotten into the room a few days before. A lot of inmates in the room knew me and knew I was a good chess player as well. They were telling me that this Parchami was beating everybody at the game, and they could not wait to see me transferred to their room so I could beat him.

Playing chess with him was not just a game for us. It was the Afghan people versus the communist regime. The room circled the two of us and watched. I won the first game to cheers in the room, but we were playing best out of three. During the second game Serbaz was patrolling the hall, and saw the big circle of inmates inside our cell. He opened the door and quietly came inside. One of the roommates alerted everybody, and quickly everyone dispersed.

As Serbaz was walking toward us I just continued playing, as I was told that my opponent was allowed to play all he wanted. Although, I was playing with my head down, pretending to be thinking about my next move. From the corner of my eye I was, in reality, curiously awaiting his reaction. As he got closer, he said hello to his friend, and did not tell me not to play. Next to my bed, another roommate was sitting on his corner of the bed still looking at our game, and that was like an insult for Serbaz.

He wanted everybody to fear him; to play dead when he was in the room. Serbaz barked at the inmate, "Look the other way. Do not look at the game."

The inmate refused, "You are not saying anything to the players, and you are telling me not to watch?" The Serbaz commanded him again to turn himself around and not to watch. He refused again. This time Serbaz got really upset and went to hit the inmate. The inmate was a close friend of mine, Mr. Baqi Khan. He was a very respectful person. I had known him for two years at that point, off and on we had met in different rooms and been roommates.

As soon as I saw Serbaz was about to throw a punch, I lost control and jumped. "Hold! Do not hit him, I will hit you if you hit him!"

Any guard in that jail had a lot of authority, but a communist guard had far more. He could do anything and no one would even ask him why. If he killed me, only then might he be questioned. So in that jail, nobody ever did something like that, especially if the guard had not done anything to you. But I would always stand up for my roommates. That is me, that is my nature, I had been beaten a lot in jail over the years for this very reason, but this time it was a little more serious. The guard was caught off guard. He never expected something like this.

For a moment he lost his mind and did not know how to react. On one hand he had to do something to retain his prestige, on the other hand he knew that he might be beaten by an inmate in a crowd of 300 others. He immediately put down his fist and straightened his back. He did not hit my friend. But he did begin to bark out loud again. "You traitors, you betrayers of this country, you shameless people, even in this jail you guys do not behave like humans!"

I went off, "You are calling us traitors? Look at the thousands of Russian soldiers; did we bring them to this country? Did we invite them?"

He shouted at me, "You thieves, you guys are just a bunch of thieves! You even steal herds of animals from the people and then take them to Pakistan to sell!"

"No, we are not taking herds to Pakistan to sell, your information is so wrong! You don't even have the basic information that meat in Kabul is way more expensive than in Pakistan, and Afghans import herds of animals to Kabul for meat. So even if we stole a herd of animals, we would never take them to Pakistan! But if we accept that we are stealing the people's herds of animals, look at you guys, stealing people's lives, stealing children's dads, women's husbands, mother's sons, people's brothers, uncles, friends, and families; treating humans like herds of animals themselves in this jail and in this country!"

He got even more upset and shouted "You guys are a bunch of killers, and you are the ones killing the Afghan people."

I shouted back. "Please! The Soviet MiGs that fly over the sky of this country every day, and bomb hundreds of villages, and kill hundreds of people every day, do not belong to us. No, these are not our jets, they belong to you and your government."

By this time every inmate in the entire room has been incited. Their circle was getting tighter around us. The guard quickly realized that he was trapped in there, and without saying anything else, left. My roommates, they just hugged me and kissed me. The adrenaline rush was still pumping through my veins. They exclaimed that, "If they send someone to take you, we all will go with you!" I know that there was not much they could do to help me. We would all be beaten and punished together. So I quickly ensured that no one would even attempt such a thing.

It was late in the day when it happened, and by dark no one had come. That evening I did not go to the washroom. I knew if I went they would take me from the hall. In the jail all inmates had a big plastic pot, their solution to the toilet situation, which we would take to the toilet to clean when it was our turn, filled from the rest of the day. That night I gave my pot to a friend to take. The following morning also I avoided going to the restrooms. But the following evening I needed to go. The toilets were in the middle of a long hall about two hundred feet away. The guards had a little room between the restrooms and ours.

As soon as I entered the hall, I saw Serbaz and three more guards just waiting there. It looked as if they had literally been waiting there all night. I ignored them and continued forward, but when I was within ten feet of them, they all moved quickly to surround me. They told me to go with them to their room without any problems.

I responded, "I have to use the restroom. Let me go and use the restroom, and then you will have no problems." They let me, and I went. When I was done, I came back to them. They took me to their room, shut the door, and all jumped on me like wild animals. Two of the guards were communists and wailed on me like I had molested their sisters, and the others came on top too in order to keep themselves from getting in trouble from the others. Just like during the interrogations, I just covered my face and forehead with my hands, and keep my thighs tied together to protect my valuable souvenirs.

After a good beating they stopped, and the Serbaz started talking again. I could tell that the last time he was frustrated more than anything that he did not get to finish what he was saying, not even that I had stood up to him. He needed the last word. In the same way he called me a traitor, a killer, a bandit, and whatever else he could think of. I responded: "You can beat me, you can punish me, you can kill me, but the reality will not change. Regardless of all the things you say, I am a political prisoner, and I have my rights. According to the law of your revolutionary government I have been held in here for five years for nothing else. As a human being we have rights, keep that in mind."

Holding me down, he continued to punch me as hard as he could. "You don't have any rights! You do what we tell you to do."

Once he stopped, I began to clean my nose, "I am not one of those little spies you have in this jail. I am not one of those so-called Mujahideen that would kill your child because you are a Parchami, and then become your "friend" while here and spy, spy, spy. I am not one of them. I will not kill a little child because his Dad is a Parchami, and I will never be reduced to a spy. I just want to do my time."

He was not sure what else to do. I clearly saw pride in the eyes of the non-communist soldiers behind him. They wanted some one like me to stand up to this guy and open his mind. Even the second Parchami guard was not saying anything, which indirectly he was distancing himself from his friend. But Serbaz was still trying to argue. He kept me in his room for another five or six hours and then, when all my roommates were asleep, they brought me back to my room to take all my belongings.

They kept all my belonging in their room, and sent me to the first floor. There was a special little area here, and they told me to stand there. They told the guards, like they had in the Khad, that I could not sleep or sit. This time there was no angel. This time I stood, for the rest of the night and throughout the following day, without sleep or food. The next night they allowed me to eat and to sit, but they did not give me a blanket. It was the month of March. I'll never forget that, because 21st of March is our New Year, and I spent that New Year standing in the freezing cold, staring at the wall, with aching legs and a screaming stomach. Kabul was always really cold in month of March, and the jail was much colder. After three days there, they sent me to block number one to stay in isolation… until today.

There in the yard trying not to think about my impending release, as the guards walked closer to me, Serbaz began giving me a closer look. He then turned his back to me and said to the guy next to him, "He is such a bastard, we should not allow him to leave the jail." My worst fears were being realized.

Soon the other man came up to me and began to ask me questions: "What was your sentence, why were you imprisoned, and what were the charges?"

I told him the sentence was for five years and that I was alleged to be a member of the Kabul University student associations. The man questioning me knew me well. His name was Sarwar Khan Heraty, and was in charge of block two. They both then walked to the office and I could see they were using the phone. I was sure they were calling the Khad, to tell them not to allow my release. All hope inside of me died at that exact moment. As they were busy talking, they began loading the buses, and the buses started rolling towards the outside of the jail. I got on, but did not believe for a second I would remain there for long. I just sat there waiting for someone to tell the driver to stop and take me off the bus. I was just waiting for someone to come running after the bus and yell, "Stop!"

But twenty minutes later we were on the main thoroughfare, the Kabul Jalalabad highway, heading west towards downtown Kabul. Slowly, I let it go—the prison, the fear, the paranoia, the pride, as the bus rolled along. Only half an hour earlier, I was in an iron casket, and now I was flying away. I could not believe it. It did not seem real.

It was so beautiful to see the outside world, which I had not done since the last bus had carted me off to Policharki. It was so beautiful to see the men, the women, the girls, the children. It was so beautiful to see the cars, the busy roads. It was so beautiful to see the plants, the trees, the animals. The only green I had seen in that prison in over four years were the tufts of wild grass in block one. There were no plants out there in the middle of the desert. Our only views of life outside that prison were the views of endless desert sands from the third floor cells...

Except, I remember, for one huge tree, fully grown about a mile away on the west side of the jail. For the first year of my incarceration I was on the floor level and was not able to see anything behind the tall walls. But after a year when they took me to the third level... and the vision of that tree was like paradise. It was the end of summer I believe, and the tree was fully green. Like my friend waving from the window, the image still haunts me. Never before had I marveled at the wonder of nature. For fifteen minutes I silently looked upon that distant tree, so emotional I thought I was not only looking at a tree, but at the creator of that tree: at the God within it. My emotions overflowed that I began to pray upon that tree. I realized then that if we looked carefully at nature, believe me, everything there is like another bible connecting to God, taking you to heaven.

Kabul was still crowded, more crowded than before. Lots of other states in Afghanistan were now so insecure that people were flocking here for refuge. Every few miles you could see a military post, with armed soldiers and tanks. Every now and then there was a military checkpoint. The highway connected Kabul to Jalalabad, then to Pakistan. It was an important highway, and posed a threat to Kabul. The pods of military presence reminded everyone of that each time they traveled it.

An hour later we were already in downtown Kabul. The buses stopped in the middle of it all in front of our most famous bank: the Pashtany Tujaraty Bank. They then told us to unload. Thousands of pedestrians were walking in every direction. I took my sheet metal box and got off the bus. Immediately greeting us were hundreds of soldiers, standing everywhere, and whenever they saw any young man in the street they would lift their guns up on their shoulders and ask to see their documents.

Again I feel myself sucked back in time: While I am standing there close to one of the guards and waiting for a taxi, I ask another bystander what they were checking for. He gives me a strange look, as if it were an everyday thing. He looks at me as if I were an alien that had just landed on a strange planet, not knowing about something as simple as a greeting or how to use money. He replies that they checked all men between 18 and, I guess, 45, so that they could round people up for the military. If someone was not a student or a government employee with proper documentation, they put him on another transport and took them straight to the army bases to give them a little training and send them off to war.

I am precisely one of those people that they are looking for. Released after four and half years in jail, just to be sent off to a military base and become a soldier for the communist regime. The only option would then be to run away, to desert your post and go to the Mujahideen, who were even more terrible than the communists. The communists were building schools finally, and sending people to get educated. They let girls and boys to go to school. They built roads, buildings, and bridges. They created jobs, but these Mujahideen, all they did was burn those schools, and force the women and girls to stay home. With men, the Mujahideen simply gave them a Quran and taught them how to kill, and how to blow things up, and how to cut people's throats.

Dozens of taxis go by and none stop for me. I was now glad I did not leave that sheet metal box in my cell as I had considered doing, even though there was nothing in it. My head was shaved, just like the soldiers heading home, and the sheet metal box was very popular with soldiers – they all had one too. No one asked me for my documents. They all were thinking I was one of those soldiers just being released from my duty.

Finally a taxi stopped and I got inside. Once inside however, I did not know where to go. I knew my mother had been living with my uncle for the past year or so, and knew the area they lived in, but I could not recall the address. I told the driver to take me to *Wazeerakbarkhan mena*. He asked me where it was in the city, I then told him to go to the *Qete-e-enzebat*. It was a military base I knew of, and from there I would be able to find my way to my uncle's.

I was, however, unaware that the *Qete-e-Enzebat* was actually the place where they were bringing all those young men they had been collecting from the streets. And right in front of the base, I paid the taxi and exited onto the street. Then, of course, I walked right up to one of the guards at the base to ask him where Dr. Azim's house was (the home of my uncle). My uncle was a physician who trained in Germany. He worked there for ten or fifteen years, but no longer practiced. He just went back to Germany a few times a year, bought a used bus, filled it with free junk, brought it back to Kabul, and it gave him enough income to live off.

The guard did not know where he lived, and luckily, did not ask any questions of me in return. He did however know of a house that was owned by a doctor, and pointed me in its direction. Still having no idea how close I was to feeding myself back into the communist machine, I followed his directions. Soon enough I recognized the house, it was indeed my uncle's.

In Afghanistan all houses had an outside wall with a door to enter the grounds. I rung the bell and saw someone from behind the window at the second floor come closer to see who it was. My uncle was overjoyed. No one knew I was coming home. So before he revealed this little miracle, my uncle walked inside and asked my mother, "How much would you pay me if I showed you your son right now?"

"Don't tease me brother, please, don't give me hard time," she responded.

My uncle replied, "I'm serious, I am not joking, tell me how much?"

That got my mother curious. Up through the window came the image of my Mom. I have never seen anybody move that fast. Down the stairs she came, throwing herself at me. Taking me up in her arms, she kissed me, and pressed me. Finally she asked me, "My son, have you escaped from jail?!?"

We talked, and talked, and talked. I was so curious, I wanted to know everything. I wanted to know where everybody was, how long they had been gone, and how they got out. How my mother had been, my relatives, my friends. My uncle soon went to the store and bought a melon, an Afghani melon. Boy that was so good: and I had missed it so much. My Mom cooked me a *chala*. The more I talked, the more I ate. After nearly five years in prison, it was like I was a little boy again who had just come home from school.

By five-thirty my uncle's wife was home. She was also a doctor, and just as shocked that here I am, stuffing my face and chattering away like I had never left. It was a very late at night before any of us went to sleep. The following day I finally got my mother to start talking about her life, and how she had managed all those years. The more she told me, the more I cry. I had not shed a tear that was not tortured out of me in nearly five years. It was perhaps the first time since I was taken that I did not hide my feelings, and it did not take more than a moment for them to come flooding back.

Mother was devastated living without her children, especially without her little son and young daughter. Every single Friday she had come, every single one for over four years. Sometimes they were unable to find a bus between the jail and the main highway, so for hours she would walk. There was only one time, a winter day, that I thought she did not show up. It was over a year ago.

I was so worried because I knew she would never miss it unless something terrible had happened. She had always to come. Sick or not, cold or hot, winter or summer, she had always to come. She wanted every week to get a letter from me to know I was still alive, and to show that she was waiting for me. She wanted to make sure that I still had a life outside those walls. From the morning until it was dark, I waited.

It was a cold night, it was snowing.

Finally I gave up.

Around seven o'clock I finally heard them call my name. I got so nervous, and started praying that everything was alright. I answered, and the guard came with the letter. At that point I was really praying it wasn't for me, to have had my mother out in the cold waiting in the snow, this late at night. But I recognized the package: it was hers. "Is my Mom still waiting outside?" I asked the guard.

"Yes she is. We have been searching for you since the morning. We were not able to find you. Each time we took your package back to her, she refused to go and begged us to try one more time. Hurry up, I need to take it back as soon as possible."

As I gave the thing to the guard, after he left, I just stood by the window and looked at the sky. It was dark, could , and the snow was coming down fast from sky. My heart was not relieved, it felt helpless. To have my mother outside in this dark, cold night, walking for hours to get to the main highway to be able to catch a bus. How was she going to get home? As I was standing by the rod iron bars of the windows and looking at the sky I was ready to make a deal with god, silently begging him to give me a pair of wings and allow me to fly out of that jail. Not to escape, but simply to accompany my mother to her home, even in exchange for my life.

For two or three days my mother and I just sat in one of the rooms. We did nothing but, really, what I had done for the last nearly five years: eating, talking and, what else? Going to the restroom! No line up, no rush, and no one complaining that I was slow!

I told my Mom and my uncle about all the restroom stories and we all laughed so much. After a couple of days my uncle told me that he needed to go to Germany and asked me if I would stay at his house for a month or so, until he returned. Once he was gone, it was only myself, my mother, my uncle's wife, and their little son Ali. The next day I sent my mother to inform one of my friends about me. She told me about the great help they had been since I had been put away.

About four of my friends, for at least three years, came every Friday to the prison with my mother to visit me. I begged them not to come, because it was extremely dangerous for them. In that jail, for some people even their brothers did not come, because there was always a chance that they would be arrested too. But every week my friends would come. Twice they arrested my friends and brought them inside the jail to investigate why they were visiting me. The following week they were there again.

Finally, after three years, they accepted the reality that they needed to stop coming. I missed my friends so much. I could not wait to see them. As soon as my mother informed one, they all rushed to come. The first day Samim was there, with Yahya and Akbar . My other close friend Bahadoor was a soccer player, and played for the national team, so he was still out of the country. But over the next few days lots of my other friends and classmates came to visit. I had very close relationship with my classmates. In another few days another close friend of mine, Pashtoon Kaker, came.

Pashtoon's oldest sister was a big time Parchami, one of the top five female communists in the country. Pashtoon's sister showed up the next day in her jeep with her bodyguards to take me to the central Khad where she had a lot of connections. This was a very different visit than my last one, though the hairs on the back of my neck stood up as we entered. This is where I was tortured during my interrogation.But I needed a letter from Khad to let me go back to the university.

Once you were arrested and sentenced for anti-government activity, you could not go back to college unless the Khad okayed it first. For me to get a letter like that on my own would have been impossible. And to be honest, a letter like that for me at that point made a difference between life and death. In but half an hour, it was in my hands. I had never looked upon such a thing with such amazement. Then she took me straight to the university, right to the headquarters of the Medical Faculty.

Once she introduced herself and told them she wanted me back at the university, no one could say no to her. They told her that they were okay with it, but it was procedure that they needed five letters from the faculty teachers to okay it on their side. That was the easy part. A lot of the teachers were anti-government. Once they heard that you were in jail for four and half years, they would automatically sign your papers. Within a couple of days I got my documents, now I could go out side with out the fear of being arrested and send to the military. Finally I had a little piece of freedom.

The next morning I went to school. University was my most favorite place on the face of the earth, I had lots of my best memories from there. But I hated it at that moment as I saw that my classmates were going to be graduating in a few months as doctors, and I was just released from jail. They had kept me in prison the entire length of the medical program. I knew at that moment that I would never return to become a full fledged doctor.

I went to stand outside the class I knew all my friends were in. Around 11:30 there was a lunch break, and as the students came out each one of them took their turn at the surprise. Every one hugged me and kissed me. They call me brave, they called me a hero. What broke my heart the most though, was that when we started in the first year, there were 220 students in my class. There were now only fifty left. Some were killed, some had left the country, some went to join the Mujahideen. I was witness to some of this myself: at one time there were up to twenty of my classmates there in prison with me. There were eight of us in one room at one point. Of the fifty, most were girls. After an hour I left with just my closer friends. That was my last day at Kabul University.

With my student card in hand there was no more threat of being detained or conscripted to the army, but instead of waiting around for the next bizarre twist in social policies I began to think about leaving the country. I loved my country, but it was not the same country anymore. To truly play a role within my nation, the choices were sparse and largely unattractive. One could join the side of the brutal, corrupt, Communist regime, or pledge allegiance to the other even more brutal and more corrupt side of the Mujahideen.

Both options meant that I would have to join in the slaughter of the poor Afghan people, and helping the Pakistanis or the Russians against my people was an act of treason in my eyes. Dying for my country did not faze me, but not for these Communists or the Mujahideen. My mother, who had waited for me, was the first one to admit that staying in Afghanistan, being who we were and believing in what we believed, was not something we could consider. The one and only time I have ever seen my mother cry was that day she began to press me to leave, pleading "I did not wait all these years, to let you stay in here and be killed."

Exactly how to leave the country was a difficult decision all by itself. All passports, required for exit, were sent to the Khad before an exit permit could be issued, and there was no way that they would allow an ex-political prisoner to leave the country with their blessing. So really, the best method of escape was through illegal means. I had never committed a true crime before this experience, but exercising my freedom of expression and travel were things I knew no government should rule against.

All the roads from Kabul to Pakistan were under the control of the Mujahideen. Crossing their paths would bring me undue risk as I did not have a beard and was easily identifiable as an educated Kabuli. Like a feeble deer at the back of the herd, their wolfish eyes would paint a target in between my eyes the second they looked upon me. They may very well kill me for sport, I thought to myself, but it was the only way. My friend Bahadour had some connections in Logar, a state just South of Kabul. The people in Logar were more educated and culturally similar to Kabul. Bahadoor spoke with a local commander there named Tamkeen – who himself was a university student before leaving to join the anti-government movement – who agreed to send me under the protection of his men to Pakistan.

But actually getting to Logar would not be simple either, as the government had posts all along the way. They stopped all the buses and, if you were not a local and were traveling to Logar, suspicion was their first response. Chances were I would end up right back in the Khad where I had started. A few days later though, Bahadoor arranged for Mateen, one of Tamkeen's cousins, to volunteer to come closer to Kabul with his bike and pick me up. As long as they went the right way, their connections within the military running those posts would allow them to pass through.

Now that I had found my way out, all there was left to do was to wait for my uncle to come back from Germany. Those days passed by in a blur of adrenaline and excitement, as I knew that one final push was needed to secure my life. Once my uncle had returned, I contacted Mateen and asked when we could leave – he said he was already waiting for me. As my uncle dropped me off in our meeting spot, I recognized Mateen as one of my fellow students at the private math and physics school I attended while in high school. Mateen was true to his word, we were able to make it past all of the security points without any hassle. A few hours later I was at Tamkeen's base in Logar Province.

This was a place the government avoided at all costs. Tamkeen took me in with open arms and we spoke for some hours in great friendship. He asked all about Policharki, and I had some questions about the Mujahideen. In response I could tell he had become unhappy with them, as he complained that he felt – as many prisoners had told me before – that the Pakistanis were simply using the Afghans for their own regional interests and gain. Tamkeen expressed to me that in Afghanistan the Mujahideen was divided between the Pakistani Mujahideen and the real Afghan Mujahideen. That the feeling within the movement was that if an Afghan mujahid went to Pakistan even once he could not be considered to be a pure mujahid.

They saw Pakistan as a place where exposure to the luxurious life their leaders had would result in the individual losing their interest in sacrificing their lives, and instead beginning to think of happiness there on earth. He told me a lot of things and shared a lot of stories about the corruptness of the Mujahideen. After some discussions, Tamkeen told me that in a few days a group of his men were going to Pakistan to take his nephews to Pakistan, as they had family in Canada, and that he wanted to make me part of that exit group. I was a bit older than most of the boys who were running the underside of Afghanistan now. Some of them weren't much older than I was before I was arrested and thrown into the Khad. These were boys, not men, in many ways. But in others, they were greater men than most men three times their age.

We left Logar in the middle of the night. It was the end of autumn, which they told me was the best time of the year to go as it was not very hot, but there was still no snow on the passes. It was three days journey to the border, and after rotting in jail for four and a half years, I knew my legs would barely be able to take the meandering, mountainous route, loose stones, and choking moon dust.

There were six of us that left Tamkeen's post, walking east towards Pakistan. Three of Tamkeen's men were armed, carrying machineguns. I asked them about their weapons, and they had plenty to say. One obvious advantage was that you could protect yourself and no one could easily rob you. The disadvantage was that between Kabul and Pakistan there were bandits who particularly liked to shoot people with machineguns, as they could sell them for up to $500 to the border area gun dealers.

By lunch the sun was high above us, but again less hot than the blistering summer heat. The three of us who were not used to the trek were exhausted. Our escorts did this journey about once a month, and spent their days walking for miles, but I and Tamkeen's nephews were gasping for air at many points. All along the way Tamkeen's men pushed us hard to move faster, as they explained to us that "the Soviet military helicopters are always on the patrol, and if they see us, they will shoot".

Eight hours in, my legs felt as they did being forced to stand in the prison. Wherever we saw a little stream of water we drank, but other than that there would be no water reserve. Going uphill was more tiresome, but moving downhill was more perilous. No part of this was easy. Our toes were blistered, but we would not stop until it was so dark that we could see nothing at all, breaking only until dawn.

We passed a lot of little villages along the way. Each little village had a graveyard. They demarcated many of the dead with flags made of the deceased garments, so you could see how many had been slaughtered in the war. At the time it was common for a family member killed by the Red Army or government soldiers, to have a white or green flag placed at the site of their grave by their families to proclaim them as a Shaheed (a martyr): telling the world they were killed in the name of the prophet Muhammad or Allah. When we Muslims passed and saw those flags, we would read a verse from the Quran and dedicate it for those Shaheeds. Tamkeen's men told me that while some of those were actually the casualties of the Soviets or the communists, unfortunately many others were instead killed in fighting among Mujahideen. But though this would normally not qualify one for martyrdom, and in fact label someone as the opposite of a martyr – as an infidel – still the flags were planted. They were planted to show their dedication to the corrupted version of Islam that was starting to morph the countryside. The very state of current affairs in Afghanistan in 2010 can be seen as starting with these little flags, mis-planted on those graves.

At around 9pm we entered a little mountainous village. The village had a small Mosque made of mud, and Tamkeen's men told us that this is where we would all sleep for the night. As we entered, we saw that the Mosque was crowded with other travelers like us. We found a little space for our group, and sat. Tamkeen's men whispered with each other and chose one to stay on guard, to make sure no one would try to kill us or take our guns. Each one had a turn, each for about two hours. That little hut reminded me again of life in prison – people crammed together in fear, simply because they would not bow down to dictatorship and violence.

Early morning: as the Azan rang out, we quickly did our prayers and began to walk again. The day before there was some food, but now it was all gone. Tamkeen's men assured us however that there would be places further down the road where we could purchase some. My feet were sore from the seventeen hours journey we had executed the day prior, but after a couple of hours I was feeling better and keeping up with Tamkeen's men pretty much the whole time. Again it was uphill, and then downhill, and up and down, and up and down. On this day though things became much more treacherous. From down below you could see it and, it didn't look so bad, we thought it would take an hour at the most to scale the pass. But as we walked and walked and walked, it would take three or four times longer.

When we came closer to the top, the pass was often covered in snow. There in the snow we would be sweating madly, and would stop to take a break. Then it was back down again, putting strain on our toes and ankles as the loose rock shifted beneath our feet. As in front of us, all the while, Tamkeen's men are bounding up and down the paths as if they were mountain goats.

After twelve hours of walking we stopped in another village. This one was bigger than the last night one, with two Mosques instead of one. We asked the locals if we could buy some food from them, but they were all short on food themselves. We took our shoes off and entered the Mosque just as the Azan was sounding, and the mosque filled up with travelers and locals. The locals all brought pieces of dried bread with them, as they knew some of the travelers would be in urgent need of food. These villagers were the poorest of the poor and did not have a lot, but took up what they could and brought it to give to people like us. That little bit of food was of great help. It was like things used to be – every Afghan helping others, ensuring the community and its visitors were taken care of. The area was closer to the Pakistani border and I cannot recall the name of the village.

As we were ready to sleep I noticed a group of Mujahideen travelers coming from Pakistan, going towards wherever their base was. They kept looking over at Tamkeen's nephews, whispering to one another. Tamkeen's nephews were teenagers: in Afghanistan some people showed interest, sexually, to boys this age. I doubt if it was serious then, but we needed to be careful. The next morning we again woke to the sound of the Azan, and after the prayers we started off again. Our toes were swelling and my shoes were far too tight as they continued to bloom. No time for complaints though. We walked another good ten or eleven hours until we finally reached the border. A few miles from the border we passed a small spring of water, and I remember very clearly Tamkeen's men telling us that this was the last source of water on the side of Afghan soil. We all drank.

For each of us about to leave our homeland, that little spring was like the Ganges to us. It was like a pilgrimage. It was the closest we got to a proper farewell to our beloved country; to all we'd known. I never in my wildest dreams had ever thought about leaving that land. I wanted to live there, and to die there. We Afghans were so proud of our poor little country. We did not know much about the outside world and we did not care much about it either. We did not have refrigerators or stoves or cars, packaged food, extra milk, all kind of dessert, gorgeous cloths and entertainment systems, but we were so happy.

As a child I never had a toy. We had our families, our relatives, our friends. We had such a good life. We thought our country was the most beautiful country on the face of the earth. I remember that in the ninth or tenth grade geography book we read that Afghanistan was so beautiful that people called it the Bride of Asia. We did not know that we were poor. We knew that we were not so rich, but not so poor at all. Even in that Policharki, I was happy. Now, with my two hands, I picked up that Afghan water, and keep washing my face over and over.

I was washing my tears. It felt like holy water. I was full, but I still took water as if I hadn't had something to drink in days. It was so tough to say goodbye to this little country of mine, and the people which I loved. I felt as if my heart had fallen into that spring and I could not go anywhere until I found it. Not without my heart; no I could not go. As I was cleaning my tears I finally stood, and we left. I felt broken; I felt pain. I felt so much guilt leaving.

I think back and I just now can finally begin to understand the meaning of my thoughts: "Would there be a salmon run for me? Where I spawn something fruitful for my country someday and for my people?" Goodbye my mother, goodbye my motherland. Goodbye the grave of my grandfather, goodbye that little dusty street where I had played. Goodbye my Pashto teacher. Goodbye that gorgeous tree behind that jail, off in the distance. I pray no one ever cut you foe wood!

Goodbye sweet melons, mulberry, sweet grapes, and delicious red-orange cherries. Goodbye my gorgeous mountains, goodbye that little mosque and goodbye that dried piece of bread. Goodbye I said to the poor people, to their rich hearts. Goodbye, I finally had to say, to that little spring: God be with you all.

My heart is still in that spring.

Later that night we reached a trifle of a mountainous border post with only a few Pakistani border police. We just shouted that we were Afghans and they let us go through. As simple as that. No grandeur, not interrogations, no gunfire. Just a shout, a wave, and we were gone. I cannot recall the name of the little area, but I believe it was Tera Mangal. There was this huge Mosque and a smallish, wealthy town. We went there for our prayers. I took some water, as we all would do, and washed it over my hands, face, feet, hair, and grabbed a small shawl we called a *patoo* which I let down next to me so it did not get wet.

It was not down for more than a minute, but when I looked back it was gone. A theft in a Mosque! That was my first experience with the rest of the world, with its culture. In Pakistan nothing was safe from leering eyes, not even in a place of holiness.

In that muddy Mosque on the Afghan side we asked those poor people if we could buy food from them. They said that they were short themselves and did not sell it to us, but at dinnertime brought some bread to us for free. That was one of the last slices of Afghani culture I would ever encounter, as I thought about where I had come to – a rich city where people were busy stealing your belongings, even as they understood that you had lost everything by leaving Afghanistan and coming here. After the prayers Tamkeen's men found a van and we chartered it to take us to Peshawar, where Tamkeen's men had a rented house and some more of Tamkeen's men were staying.

We did not reach it until late at night. The following morning I met the rest of Tamkeen's men. There were a few of them, all high school kids, that had left school to fight against the Soviets. They told me then however that, after a couple years, they finally realized that it was not a real Jihad they were a part of. They thought now that most of the Mujahideen were worse than the communists, and decided to quit. Now they had applied to some European embassies for refugee status and were waiting to hear back about their applications. The boys were from Kabul, and when they heard that I was a political prisoner and had led the Kabul University Student Association, the affinity of brothers at arms blossomed immediately. I told them some things about my trials, but mostly wanted to hear from them—every Afghan had such a story to tell in those days, a romantic and bloody tale that novelists could never truly replicate.

I stayed with them for two days before we went out into Peshawar, which was now filled with Afghan ex-patriots. I thought it was important for me to see, how miserable life was for the Afghans there, so far from home and in a hostile world that spit upon their presence. We took a little taxi and went for a good drive. For hours we drove, as they pointed to hundreds of Afghan women begging for food on every street corner. Some had a small child with them, others had their whole family begging alongside them.

They showed me Afghan men too, standing on the corners begging for food. I asked Tamkeen's men why they were not working, and they told me that some did, but there was nothing to do in Pakistan. Pakistanis were largely poor themselves, and would not even hire you to clean their house for a speck of food. Many European and American companies had put down roots in Pakistan just to help these Afghans with jobs, especially sporting goods and clothing companies, but the Pakistanis simply kept the jobs for themselves. Some international aid agencies also opened plants so that Afghans could create their own products, such as the high demand Afghani rugs, but Pakistanis would soon take over the plants and only hire locals. It was too difficult for the agencies to control it, and to be honest, they had difficulty distinguishing between the Pashtun Afghans and Pashtun Pakistanis.

The Pakistanis also competed for refugee status with the Europeans and Americans. There was a black market, of all things, selling approved applications written out for Afghans to Pakistani families instead. They would steal the applications, or just copy them, and distribute them among their own. They changed the addresses and the poor Afghan family simply received a fake letter from the Pakistanis, who had just stolen their information, that they have been rejected, while a Pakistani family had already gone to United States or Europe in their place.

Those corners in Pakistan tore me in half. I had never seen people begging before, not like that. Now our proud nation was being brought to Pakistan, with the promises of a better life, only to become beggars. I asked Tamkeen's men if the UN was helping. But they replied that every penny was soaked up elsewhere, and described a situation identical to the one I'd heard in prison. All the aid went to the Pakistani government. First the Pakistani officials looted as much as they wanted, then perhaps a dime from a dollar went to the seven Mujahideen groups. The leaders on the top of those groups looted as much as they could at that point, and gave the rest to their commanders.

By the time that helps reached the Mujahideen itself, it had been reduced to a few machineguns, and a minor amount of pay. The refugees could do nothing but live in the camps, in those little tents, dirty and hot like hell, with maybe a bag of flower, a can of oil, and a little rice: just enough to keep them alive. Thousands of refugees died each year because of the conditions (which were anything but sanitary), hunger, and the heat. They told me that Pakistanis not only stole all the aid, but that the local police looted anything else left on the Afghan refugees everywhere they went.

They recognized the Afghans from their light skin and the robes and stopped them whenever they pleased. They believed that if you could afford to have a clean robe, it meant you had at least a few rupees to give them as a bribe to let you go. The aim of the police was not to check your documents for real, because they already knew we were legal as the authorities quickly issued each of us a small card, they simply wanted to imply that yours was a fake and that only a bribe would let you out of their grasp.

Those few rupees would almost always be the money they had for their child's food, nothing more. No wonder we all had to beg. If you were lucky enough to get a few rupees from others, you had to split that with the police. The Pakistani government loved to see as many Afghans as possible in Pakistan because the more refugees there were the more aid would flow into their country, translating into millions of dollars for corrupt government officers in the upper ranks of Pakistan and bribes for the local police. We Afghans did not see or feel what those high ranking government Pakistanis were doing, but we definitely felt the oppression of the local authorities. They stole every last rupee from our pockets after their government left us with almost nothing. When the police asked you for your documents, automatically an Afghan knew it meant it was time for a bribe, otherwise you would end up in prison.

Many of them would carry around a small bag of marijuana, and tell you directly that if you did not bribe them, they would place it in your pocket and arrest you on drug charges. On the other hand the Afghan women, even young girls, were frequently abducted and sold into the sex trade. Many of these were abducted by the police for trafficking – they even stole some boys for organ harvesting. In the best of cases the child would be lucky enough only to lose one kidney and be let go a few days later. Seeing such wounds on a child left a deeper wound upon your soul. In the worst of cases, only a torn open corpse would be found, or they would simply disappear forever. It was as if we had left Heaven, as warlike as it was, and entered Hell.

It was too late for these Afghans to go back, as they very soon began to yearn for the opportunity to return and work for the communists. The Mujahideen were everywhere; it was total chaos. Nowhere was it safe. Applying for refugee status meant leaving yet another country for somewhere more secure – getting approved as a refugee in Europe, Canada, or the United States was literally like hitting the jackpot. We were okay though, for now, as the taxi window obscured the view of the police and they could not tell if we were Afghan or Pakistani... yet.

I asked Tamkeen's men why people didn't demonstrate against the Pakistani government, or the seven Mujahideen leaders. They told me that the seven leaders of the Mujahideen were seven vicious dogs in the hands of ISI. To complain in Pakistan against the Mujahideen or the Pakistani government, meant that they would quickly mark you as a Kabul government agent, leading to your arrest. Once they arrested you, you were gone. Even in Afghanistan they would let you out of their jails, but not here – thousands would simply enter and die. There was no law and order in this Pakistan, in this place where the entire world was sending their aid for dear, sweet Afghanistan.

They told me that all seven Islamic groups had their own torture places and detention centers. The way they tortured people in Pakistan was ten times worse, at the very least, than the Afghan torture I had endured at the Khad. At least in Afghanistan there was a government that felt responsibility, across the border it was a chaos. Nobody would even admit that they had arrested you. And hopefully you would not witness such an abduction, or else they would look to eliminate you too.

There were tens of thousands Afghans missing in Pakistan, all arrested and killed by the Pakistani puppets. It was not only the ones with complaints that the Mujahideen were arresting and killing though; they became indiscriminant and impulsive. If they did not like your beard, they would kill you. Besides arresting Afghans, assassinations of Afghans was a common thing in Pakistan. Hundreds lost their lives each month. Even some of the Mujahideen commanders in Afghanistan who were not doing exactly what the ISI told them to do were targeted when they returned to Pakistan looking for their rations. Thousands of Mujahideen commanders died like this. If you disobeyed an order, no matter how inhumane – like blowing up a dam or slaughtering a schoolgirl, you were targeted.

At the end of the third day I told my new Afghan friends that I was leaving for Islamabad, the capital of Pakistan. The next morning they took me to the bus station and we said goodbye. I think it was a few hours' drive. When I arrived in Islamabad, I took a taxi and gave him an address I had been given. In another fifteen minutes he dropped me off at the addres. I knoced at the door and the boy inside shouted with surprise.

Baser Hakimie, one of my closest school friends, was staying here. We were together at the high school. Baser and Nasser were very rich in Afghanistan. In Afghanistan, if your house had toilets and sinks, and an electric pump, and of all things a car, you were really rich. During some of my tougher days in high school I spent time with them. I always helped them with their homework. Their family was extremely happy to see me with their boys, showing them how to succeed.

I remember that often when I would stay over at their homes, we would stay up all night laughing. Baser's older brother was a joker. He would make us laugh so hard our backs would hurt and our jaws would seize up. He was the one who had given me this address after he visited me once I was released from prison. We hugged each other and held tightly for like a minute. Baser was crying out of joy. He was a member of our organization too, and was himself in the jail for a few months. As we entered his wife ran and greeted me. Baseer's sister Mehrafzoon, her husband Abraham, they all quickly brought me tea and started cooking.

Baser now had a sweet little girl named Ghizal; she was just like a doll. His sister had two little sons. I knew all of them from Kabul except the kids, who were not born yet when I was put away. Baser and Abraham were married to each other's sisters. Baser now lived in a little room with his wife, daughter, sister, brother-in-law, and their kids. They had tough lives in Islamabad, a far cry from their near opulence in Kabul.

For money they went to a place which sold used Japanese blankets, bought a few, then brought them home to hand wash them, dry them, and then brush each one for a couple hours to make them shine. Then, when they looked like new, twice a week there was a flea market, where they went to sell them. They made enough to eat and pay the rent for their little room.

While we were having dinner I was thinking about where to go for the night. To be honest, I had only a few hundred kaldar (Pakistani money), which was practically nothing. And I could not sleep there. In Afghanistan, when you are sleeping with your wife, even your brother does not sleep there. At the very least their situation put two brothers and sisters together. In no way would I allow myself to sleep in there. As it got dark, I said goodbye, to go. They asked me where. I replied that I would find a little hotel or something around the area. They told me that in no way would they allow me to go anywhere. I swore I would not stay there, but they insisted as if I was their blood brother.

As much as I insisted, they held my little package, and said, "You are a brother to all of us, and an uncle to our kids, in no way will we let you go." To make a long story short, they held me there. I felt so embarrassed to sleep in their little room, but at the same time so honored that they treated me that closely. They kept me there for two weeks, and they treated me like a guest of honor.

As soon as I reached Baseer's home I send a message for my Mom. She wanted to wait for me to reach Pakistan before she fled, because, as she said, "if this government catches you, you will be back in jail, and I will need to stay until you are done." As soon as she got my message she left Kabul by bus. She was an older lady, so it was much easier for her to take a bus to the Pakistani border, then walk to the other side and take another bus to Peshawar. I told her that once she was there she could send us a message, and I would go bring her to Islamabad.

Islamabad, my friends were telling me, was booming. The Afghan aid money stolen from international coffers was turning into businesses, buildings, cars, theaters, new cities, and hundreds of new Mosques in those cities and a better life for those that lived there. They told me that a few years prior Islamabad was dirty and poor, but that now it was a city with life. The building which Baser had rented in was a modern building; it even had a modern sewer system and a fire place as a source of heat. My first time to see a modern fireplace. The room was one of the three bedrooms in that house rented by different people. But, of course, everything was built with a Pakistani twist.

One night after we went to sleep I woke up after only a few hours, and felt like I was dying. I was unable to breathe, with severe nausea and dizziness. Something was terribly wrong. I knew I needed to run out of the room. Try as I might to move my body, I was not able to turn my body. I tried to shout and wake the room, but I was not able to shout. I was just vomiting and could barely turn my body. It was worse than any night I had spent on the floor in the Khad. Finally I crawled to the door and slid it open. The smell of gas from the fireplace was strong – I was not used to this smell in Afghanistan, so I noticed it far sooner than anyone else.

It took me a minute to be able to shout to the others, but no one responded. I rushed back into the room and shouted as loudly as I could, shaking everyone awake. Some were able to crawl outside, some I pulled, and it took all of us ten to twenty minutes to return to normal. We calmed ourselves down and eventually reentered the room, however returning to sleep was difficult. Although we turned the fire place off, every couple of hours or so I woke up for a short moment in a panic. We had almost died, the room of us, out of nowhere. Four and a half years in jail, the torture, sneaking past three militaries – the Red Army, the Afghan communists, and the Mujahideen – without a moment like this, only to leave Afghanistan and die in Pakistan silently beside the families of two brothers in that small, little room filled brilliantly with life.

In prison I knew I wanted to write a book, and prayed to God that I would not die so that he would let me do it. But now, even after enduring five years of fear and despair under the communists, I knew that I had to write about the greater evil at hand – the ISI and their puppet extremists.

Two and half weeks after I reached Baseer's my mother mes-
saged me from Peshawar. Baser and I took a bus to bring her to
Islamabad. With the same grace and generosity, they allow my
mother to stay with us. His sister insisted, as did his wife, that Baser
would be brokenhearted if we left. That is how much love he had,
and how strong an Afghan man he had become.

The plan was now to go to New Delhi, India. A week and a half
later we packed for Lahore, the Pakistani border city. I cannot recall
how many hours drive it was, but I believe it was over five. We said
goodbye to our dear friends and left. Baser, my friend, came along
with us. He wanted to make sure everything went alright. We did
not have passports, but knew that a fake one could be bought just
about anywhere in Pakistan. For a hundred dollars a smuggler asked
us to meet us at a specific time and place for him to get us past the
customs agents. There were about twenty of us, and even though our
passports were fake, they already knew we were coming and the first
custom agents let us go.

We met some Afghans at the border that had experience with the
Pakistani and Indian border agents and warned us to keep only small
bills on us for bribes and to hide the rest of our money, or else it
would all be gone within a few minutes of entering the border. True
enough, as we crossed the border almost every person working there
held us up and threatened to send us back if we did not give them a
bribe. I felt as if we were a swarm of grasshoppers under attack by a
hungry flock of birds, preying on us. You gave them small bills, but
they knew you had more.

On the Indian side of customs, the same game continued. Once
again they preyed upon us the same way. By the time we were done,
some of us did not have a penny left to buy a bus ticket to go to New
Delhi, where the UN office for Afghan refugees was. I think our
mother believed we were two of those unfortunates, not able to buy
a bus ticket for New Delhi, but I had a surprise. Hidden away in my
toothpaste, was two hundred dollars. And with that money, I bought
tickets for the two of us, in addition to all those who lost everything
at the border.

Now the goal was to get to New Delhi where the UN was giving
each Afghan refugee about five hundred rupees per month in addi-

tion to medical care. Direct payment, right into your hands, free of the grubby paws surrounding the aid in Pakistan. When we arrived in New Delhi it was around three in the morning. We took a taxi and gave them the address of where we needed to go. Half an hour later we were knocking the door. Again, we are there to surprise old family and friends. "Who is there?" asked the woman.

I answered, "Shafie."

In a rush my aunt opened the door. We hug and kiss, and my cousins, three little girls, wake up. It was like Christmas each time, these greetings again and again at the door as we smuggled ourselves across Asia. I had not seen my aunt in five years, who was always the closest of all our relatives. This was my mother's younger sister, and my mother loved her like one her own children, maybe more. I remember that when we were in Kabul the only people who could come to our house without restrictions were her kids – all seven of them. The only people with which my Mom was not hesitant with her food was them. My Mom even washed their clothes and took them to the public baths on occasion. My aunt had to leave Afghanistan with her kids and was now living in Delhi, but a year ago had spent all her money to hire a smuggler to send four of the older kids (between the ages of eleven and seventeen) to Canada, where they have been accepted as refugees. She and the rest of family were waiting for the kids to sponsor them.

India was far different than Pakistan. First, although the Indian government had a close relationship with Moscow and the Afghan Government, the Afghan refugees had freedom and nobody abused them. Secondly, the Indian government had no interest in robbing the aid coffers of Western powers. The United Nations had its own office there though, where they were helping the Afghan refugees with enough for rent and food. And the police in India were not targeting us, so the money was not seeping away in the tides of greed as it was the entire route there.

The Indian people were not stealing our documents from the embassies to send their own relatives instead of us. No one was abducting our little kids to harvest their organs. No one was abducting our little girls for slavery. No one was picking our people from the street corners and taking them to a secret jail for torture. No one was disappearing. Our kids could go to school with their kids, while in Pakistan Afghan kids were not able to attend the Pakistani schools. India was far more beautiful, people were more open-minded. India was far more advanced; the houses were modern. The only thing was that most of the time it was just so crowded and noisy. Half the time anybody was driving they seemed to be pressing on the horn.

As soon as we arrived in New Delhi, we went to the refugee office to apply for help. We then went to the American Embassy to apply for a refugee visa. Every three months an immigration judge came from the US to India and interviewed everyone who had applied. When we arrived we were told that it was kind of late to see the judge that was coming in one month, because the papers took a little longer to process. So we had missed the first one after we arrived, but would be able to see a judge in four months.

When the appointment came the judge read the portions we had written about ourselves and our situation and had some questions for us. When he noticed that my mother's whole family was in America, including her little ones, he showed a lot of sympathy. It only took a month to receive our visa, along with an airline ticket out of India and all our expenses paid. It was the most miraculous thing I had ever seen. I had never imagined this kind of help existed in the world. The flight connected through Hong Kong, which was a marvel in itself. The next day we were in San Francisco.

This final reunion is something I can still barely bring myself to think about without crying. The only ones missing at the airport were my oldest sister Parween, who was living in San Diego and had plans to come in a few days, and Rona, my younger sister, who was in the Hospital. They told me she was there to give birth to her first son: Massieh (Masaia), just two days before our arrival.

The next morning when my older brother went to work he took me with him. He had a small business selling single roses to the convenience stores. This was my first time in America: imagine that in Policharki my dream was to have a restroom someday, to sit without anyone bothering me, and now it felt like such dreams were something so far out of mind for the people here that if I told anyone they would just laugh. At lunchtime my brother stopped at a Kentucky Fried Chicken. In Afghanistan chicken meat was the most expensive kind you could get. We did not even have farm-raised chickens. I remember once in a while when we were very lucky Mom would butcher a chicken, one for all of us.

Boy, just one a shred of it made it to our bowls, but it was so good. In America people were eating chicken even without rice or bread. I doubt if our King had even stopped to think of eating chicken all by itself! I was so upset at my brother: he was pulling the skin off, and not eating it. "No, no, never do that, give it to me: that is the most delicious part of the chicken!" I ate all of mine and all of his skin.

America was so amazing to me, unlike anything I could have ever imagined before I arrived. The houses were beautiful, the cars were gorgeous, the buildings - the civilization. The American people were different too. A lot of them said hello as they passed by you, mere strangers, with a smile on their lips. They were more beautiful, better dressed. And do you know what the biggest difference was? So many cars, everywhere, and all of them so quiet. In Afghanistan we did not have a lot of cars, but in India, honking was the driver's first language. A single honk, a double honk, a triple honk, a double and a single, a double-double, a triple-triple, and a long continuous honk, all had their own meanings. Sometimes a driver would just keep the horn pressed down and drive.

They could curse, they could thank, they could give suggestive comments to a bypassing woman, they could fight, and all kinds of other things, just with the use of their horn. India was the noisiest place I have ever been. In America there were so many more cars but compared to India there was no noise at all. My brother told me that honking in America is an insult to other drivers. The only time you honk is if someone is getting dangerously close to you, and maybe once in a while for other purposes.

I remember we were on a little highway, which connected the city of Hill Top to the city of Concord when I started to see signs that said "Help Wanted". I got curious and asked my brother what that meant. He explained to me if someone wanted to hire somebody, for a job, they posted that sign outside their door. Wow... that was so difficult for me to even imagine. What a fair and polite way to hire someone. In Afghanistan first of all you would never see such a sign; people needed to dig for a job. One needed to go door to door or office to office in order to see if they could track one down. And second, no one would ever tell you that they needed your help, it was always *you* that needed *their* help.

On my third day I was in the city of Hill Top on San Pablo Avenue and my brother stopped at a Shell gas station to get some gas. There in the window I saw the sign again, asking for help. My brother knew I would be so happy if I could find a job, and he told me that he would go inside and ask the owner what kind of help he needed. He came back and told me that they needed someone to pump gas and collect the money. Sounds easy to me, I thought. He told me that the owner was going to come out to interview me, because he needed someone urgently. So that he could mask the fact I did not speak English, my brother said he would speak for me and told me to just say yes or no.

A moment later the owner came and talked with me, but it didn't take long for him to pick up on our ruse. And yet, lo and behold, he appeared to still be okay with taking me on. So he asked me if I understood American money. I said yes. He then put his hand in his pocket and pulled a handful of change from his pocket. He showed it to me and asked me to prove it: "Show me which one is a dime, a nickel, a quarter, and a penny." I did not know which was which. All I knew was the paper dollar. I could not do it, so he could not take me on. Yes that was my first ever job interview, how easy it was but I failed! At home everybody laughed and laughed, and showed me what I had done wrong. I remember how confusing it was that a nickel was bigger than a dime, but was worth less.

For two months I was jobless. Since I was a refugee there was welfare, where they would hand me some cash and food stamps. When I went to stores I saw that everybody was paying in cash and handing over my food stamps made me feel incredibly embarrassed. I felt as if I was cheating somebody – so young and healthy, with welfare in my hand. I felt like the beggars on the street corner in Pakistan.

Two months later my brother told me that he had found me a job at a convenience store about thirty miles away. The store owned by a Pakistani. The good thing was that I already had my driver's license and learned to drive since I arrived. My family had an old Chevy Nova that was only for grocery shopping and wasn't really needed. My second interview went much better and I got the job. The store was in Oakland and very busy. A grocery store with gas station- Arco Am Pm. I was ecstatic – so proud.

My job started around eight in the evening and the shift lasted until about six the next morning. I first swept the parking lot clean, then cleaned all the toilets outside and inside. I then filled up the cooler, and after that, I arranged the shelves and stocked them. The problem was that I still did not speak English, and more than that, I did not know anything about 95% of the products. When I stocked the cooler, the only drinks I knew were water, milk, Coca Cola, and orange soda. All the rest were new to me.

This was how I learned about America. The owner showed me everything I needed to know, and I start to call him Chief. It took me a month to figure out all the products, or at least what I thought they were. The moment I did, Chief then put me on as a cashier; I think somebody had quit and he needed someone to do the job quite urgently. I told him that I had no experience, and that I did not know how to use the machine nor speak to the customers. But he knew my reaction before I gave it, and patiently explained that he would train me.

That same day I was trained. Boy, that was tough, but since he was there, I was not afraid. The following day he put me back on cashier after I was done my routine. He stayed with me until 11pm, and then went home. I was literally about to faint. The store was located in a rough neighborhood, and during the nightshift we closed the door and served the customers through a little window. That was a nightmare for me. When the door was open, the customer came inside, picked up what they needed, and all I had to do was ring them up. At night they came to the widow and would ask me for this or that, when I still barely understood what half the things in the store were.

Believe me, when I stocked the cooler, I only knew the products visually but now people would have to tell me the name of the products and would expect me to bring it to them in rush, without my being able to communicate with them, which was a double-sided coin at the end of the day. The negative thing about not knowing the language was that I would get embarrassed, but the good thing was that when the customers got upset (and boy did some of them get upset) and cursed at me, I had no idea what they were saying to me, so I still smiled at them.

In a couple days though, I learned something incredibly useful. The owner's wife, who had almost the same problem as I did, had a trick. If she did not know something she would always ask the customer, "What do you mean by (x)?" For example, if someone said 'do you have Mars bar,' or 'can you give me a Mars bar,' she would reply 'what you mean by Mars bar?' Then they explained it and she handed it over or showed it to them.

A few nights later, around eleven at night, I had a line at the window. The next guy in line is a well-dressed, nice, and clean gentleman. When it was his turn, he very quietly said, "Give me a pack of condoms."

I had no idea what "condoms" is. I asked him loud and clear, "what do you mean by condom?"

He whispered back, "Condom man, condom!" I asked him again what he meant, of course, as I had no way of knowing what he was talking about.

Instead of explaining it to me, he just tells me again, "Condom man, condom."

I repeated again, this time more clearly, "What do you mean by condom?"

This time I saw the colors of his checks turn a little red, and the embarrassment in his eyes, as he repeats "Condom, condom."

I asked him again what he meant by "condom".

We never had condoms in Afghanistan, otherwise I would definitely not have had seven sisters and brothers! This time the people standing in the line behind him were all laughing, and he is kind of upset. He, this time, makes a little hole with his left hands fingers and, with his right middle finger, started penetrating the hole repeatedly. I got really upset, believing he was telling me 'fuck you' or something, but the good thing was that I did not know how to say the same thing back. In Afghanistan, if someone cursed you like that, there would be a big fight, but quickly someone from behind him jumped in the front and, with his hand, directed me to the end of the store. There he told me to sit and look down, right and left, and right, finally directing me to pick the pack, and I brought it.

This sexy guy knew exactly where we were keeping our condoms!

It was a blue pack of Trojans. Everybody laughed and applauded for me.

That was not the only thing, a few nights later, a guy asked me to give him a Dr. Pepper while standing in a line of similar boisterousness. Again I was confused. Now, I knew 'doctor', in fact, I was supposed to become one, and I knew pepper, I could not eat without it, but I did not know 'Dr. Pepper.' My boss had an Indian friend who was a doctor and came in to pay Chief a visit every now and again. He often asks me to get him a cold beer. I quickly thought of him.

However, I was not sure if his name was "pepper" or not. In India sometimes they had quite strange names, and half of me was telling me that the costumer was looking for the boss's friend, so maybe his name was pepper! The other half was telling me that maybe he needed to buy some pepper. I did not want to look stupid, so I said, "Sir, doctor is gone home but we have pepper!"

Four or five months later I left San Francisco for Los Angeles. I wanted to do what my older brother did. When I talked to my brothers about it, they advised me not to go to LA, not yet. They told me that I needed to go to school, learn English, work more and save some money. Then, once I knew the society a little better, I could do business. But I did not accept that. I insisted that I was a quick learner and that I wanted to go.

My younger brother Rahmath came with me to help me rent a room and find some suppliers. He was with me for a few days and then went back, as he had his own business to take care of. I did rent a room in New Port and a little garage in a different place so I could wrap my roses. I then went and bought all the supplies I needed.

I wrapped my first batch of fresh roses and was supposed to go out the following day to sell my roses in the retail stores. The problem was that I still could not speak English, beyond just enough to introduce myself to someone and offer the product I had. Things were always easier when you're dreaming them up in your head, rather than going out and actually doing them. I probably would have listened more to my brothers if I had known how I would feel that day, in that little garage, in Los Angeles. I was so nervous to go out and start my business. The whole night I rubbed my back and brainwashed myself, saying "yes you will be able to do it. It is easy." But deep inside another voice was keep telling me "No, it is not. You better pack and go back home, to momma" I spent the whole night Brainwashing myself and practicing my sentences for the following day's sales job.

The next day I put the roses in the trunk of my car and left to talk to the store managers. For three and a half hours, I could not get up the courage to go in and talk to anybody. Finally, at about 11:30, I stopped at a store with a Mexican food restaurant attached to it. It was very crowded inside. There I stood in the line with a vase and a bunch of my roses. When my turn came I asked the cashier, "Can I talk with the manager?" This was an exact sentence my brother wrote for me. So just like a parrot I mimicked it. The guy started speaking. In my notebook, my brother said the manager will say 'I am the manager,' or they will call the manager, and then I was to continue with my next sentences.

But this guy said something that was not in my notebook. He said "speaking," but that was all I got out of it. I nervously repeated, "Can I talk with a manager?" A Mexican background himself, he figured out my problem, and as a joke he held up his shirt, "This is the manager." This time I understood. I offered my product, but very nicely he refused to buy, "Because we are more like a restaurant, it will not work for me, but I like the idea."

Although he did not buy from me, he encouraged me a great deal. So I got a little more courage and stopped in the next one, who bought from me. And the next one, and the next one, and the next one. At the end of that day I had a dozen accounts. The next day I opened more accounts, and the next day even more. Soon I had enough accounts to generate some income and at the same time work on opening new accounts. I opened more than one hundred very quickly, but was not making enough money to sustain my life. I was working six days a week, between 12 to 14 hours a day, but not enough income to really pay for everything, because a lot of my roses were dying too quickly in the heat of my car. Three or four months later I realized that I could not afford to pay my rent, as I was sending my family four hundred and fifty dollars a month to help.

We did not want our mother and young siblings to collect the housing from the government. They were already collecting welfare, but we felt responsible for taking care of everything else. We could not afford to pay for everything, but this was our mother; we needed to do something. In Afghanistan your Mom and Dad take care of you as long as they can, but when they are not able to anymore, it is your moral responsibility to do the same for them. Now, although in America, we would feel ashamed if we let our Mom go and collect her rent from the government: who would we be then? So every month I paid as much as my two other brothers – Khalil and Rahmath – did towards the family. Between that and my rent, I couldn't afford both, so I talked with my landlord, explained my situation, and left. But I was not homeless. I had my Chevy Nova!

I was now using my car for picking up my roses, delivering them, and at night time, I would go to Huntington Beach, my most favorite place, park my car somewhere with an ocean view and sleep in the back seat. I loved it. To this day I always laugh and say my first house had an ocean front. The only problem I had was where to take a shower. Sometimes I would take a bucket of cold water and wash myself in the garage where I stored my roses. Sometimes I would go to the beach and use the standing showers. But the problem was that when I went there and soaped myself up, I thought that everybody knew I was without a real home. I did not want to look homeless. In the morning I would go to the McDonalds or a fast food store and shave my beard quickly, and that embarrassed me even more. Other than that I was so happy.

Since I was living in my car, I did not have a phone, so my family could not get a hold of me. A few times a week though, I would use a public phone to call. On one call my older brother Khalil told me that a friend of mine had called them from an American detention center and needed some help. They told me he was Mustafa Rawani. Oh, I know Mustafa, he was my classmate at Kabul University, I said. He was then, more importantly, my roommate in Policharki.

The story I always remembered him by was that in prison Mustafa got a toothache. For a week he suffered from the pain, before finally the jail physician sent someone to bring him over, during one of his visits that were twice a week. He was the only physician for twenty-five or thirty thousand inmates. He was not a dentist, but he acted as our dentist too.

He removed the tooth with a pair of pliers, with no anesthesia. Afterwards he was still in a lot of pain, which we thought was just from the operation. But soon enough we discovered that the doctor had removed a healthy tooth, and that the bad one was still there. A few days later the doctor returned and went in again. Two days after that he was still in pain, because the doctor made the same mistake again.. We couldn't help but laugh and give him a hard time, telling him not to see that doctor again otherwise, one by one, he would pull all his teeth out except the bad one! Finally, one of our friends took a string and removed it himself.

When in India I met Mustafa again and even then he and I were making jokes about his tooth, and were both laughing a lot. I knew Mustafa was desperately trying to find a way to leave India and go to America or Canada. He had a couple thousand dollars and was looking for a smuggler to send him to one of those countries. He had finally made it to America, but was in a detention center and needed an attorney to represent him. In those days if you were an Afghan most countries (especially America, Canada, and European countries) would not deport you, but he needed an attorney just to make sure.

We did not have nearly enough to help, but my brothers worked really hard to put together three thousand dollars and hired some-body for him. Soon Mustafa was out of jail, but now he was looking for a place to live. I was the only one he had, but me, I was living in my car. A couple days later my brothers bought him a bus ticket and sent him over. Now my Chevy Nova was also my guest house. During the day Mustafa went with me to the stores and at night we both slept in our little ocean view room. A few weeks later I was able to find him a job in a liquor store. Mustafa's English was better than mine, and I knew he would be able to hold down a regular job. I just told him that Dr. Pepper was not a doctor, it was a drink, like Coca

Cola, because we both knew what Coca Cola was. I told him about condoms too and a few other things I had learned the hard way, and of course I told him about my Pakistani boss's wife's trick, with a Pakistani accent, of course "What do you mean by condom?!" Other than that, I thought that he would be fine.

In a few months, in search of a better place for my business, I moved to Seattle and established the same business in Oregon and Washington states. This time I grew bigger and was able to buy a few little trucks and hired a few people to work under me. In a few years I found some new products and added to my income. Although I had employees, I never stopped getting out there, selling and delivering myself. For the first fourteen years I believe I worked twelve to fourteen hours a day, six days a week. For two years, twice a week I was starting at 12 midnight and going until 8 or 10 pm the next night. Twenty or twenty-two hours straight.

Once someone asked me how I became successful in America as a refugee, when he was American born still had to work for me; he just didn't understand why. I told him that when I came to America I had so many disadvantages, I was so desperate to find a place to sleep better than my car, so that disadvantage became an advantage and, I said to him, perhaps your advantage has become your disadvantage. It is a problem that can strike anybody, anywhere – though most Americans are incredibly smart and hardworking. I was so lucky that I came to America; I always thank god and believe me when I look at the flag of this great nation each star in that flag shines like a million stars to me! Many people in America, they do not know how lucky they are.

During all these years in America wherever I went I found the Afghan community and tried to become friends with them. In my first year in Seattle I saw that the Afghan community was still demoralized and fearful of the Ikhwanis (Muslim extremists). I did my best to change that. In the beginning even at the weddings one of the Ikhwanis would do the Azan and everyone had to run and do a collective prayer, right in the middle of the ceremony. These kind of collective prayers were not for a pure religious purpose, it was designed to force people to stand behind the extremists through intimidation. It was a reminder that they were in charge. Normally in a wedding hall Afghans miss a collective prayer and then do it at home later, but when you put them in the situation where they have to do it, they will disrupt even their wedding in order not to show disrespect to Islam.

This was in the 1980s. Even then, they were developing an air of authority for themselves, as the purest of the pure. I took a chance by not moving when they told me to. I led by example, letting them know that they could not influence me. Enough others followed, and soon the extremists stopped showing up. They soon understood that they were isolating themselves, not the other way around. Leading the religious stuff was the main way for them to control people. Once they'd lost that, they'd lost everything. I gradually created a strong opposition to them and gradually encouraged people against them. In those days the extremists were not called terrorists, because they were only killing our poor Afghan friends back home. At that time the Afghan War was "Charlie's War" and even in America the extremists were popular.

I remember I was still in Los Angeles (1984-1985) when a group of Mujahideen leaders came to United States, invited to visit President Reagan at White House. The leader of the group though, Mr. Hekmatyar, refused to see Reagan, as if it was a sin for him to see the leader of the free world. And this guy was the biggest receiver of American money and weapons in Pakistan. No one in America cared about that. No one even asked about why this guy, who we were sending tens of millions of taxpayer dollars, was so hateful towards us, refusing an invitation from the White House. A lowlife like Gulbudeen Hekmatyar was refusing to meet President Reagan! Perhaps at that time the Pakistanis told the CIA that this was only on the surface, and that deep inside he was "with you guys". In fact, the Pakistanis trusted the Gulbudin more than other Mujahideen leaders, because he was so hateful of America! That way America could not be in direct relationship with Afghan people, and they hade to use the ISI.

It was in America that I began watching the games that the Pakistanis were playing: Gorbachev, the new leader of the Soviet Union, was begging the Mujahideen leaders to form a government so that the Soviet troops could leave Afghanistan, but Pakistan was not allowing their Mujahideen leaders to do so. The Pakistanis did not want the war to end and for the aid money to stop flowing. I always say that a good politician is the one can see through the current times; that can clearly see the next ten years, the next twenty years, the next fifty years, and chooses policies to benefit the long term, not policies that look useful for this particular moment. In America Afghanistan became a momentary policy, with no long term vision.

In the end, Gorbachev could not hold on anymore for the so-called Afghan Mujahideen to form a government. They had to realize that the Mujahideen was not a constructive force. The only training they were getting was how to destroy, how to demolish, how to blow things up, and they were now masters of the craft. To this date they have been able to do nothing else.

It was 1989, I believe in February, I was watching the news when I came home from work. The news was showing the last of the Soviet troops crossing the Afghan borders into Uzbekistan. General Gromove was crossing the so-called friendship bridge for the last time. It was an emotional moment for me. I watched, and tears fell from my eyes. I thought of the weasel in the Khad, maybe for the first time in years. I remember him cackling as he belittled and read my poem aloud, to an eighteen year old boy, "Maderam ber marge be taboot farzandat manal." I remembered him smashing my head against the wall as he shouted, "Do you think that we are going to lose the war in Afghanistan, and have you guys celebrate our defeat?" While I was dying of pain he answered for me, "No, no we will not lose the war, because the Red Army of the great Soviet Union is supporting us!" I had not thought of him in years, but at that moment he was the one I truly wanted to be with. I wanted to hold his ears and hit his head against the wall, and tell him "Where is your Red Army now, ha? Where are they now?" I had long forgiven those that perpetrated crimes against me, but in that moment, I felt a renewing fury in my soul. That fury may well have been stirred by my suspicions of what was soon to come for Afghanistan – suspicions that the following decades proved correct.

As soon as the Soviet troops left Afghanistan and left their puppet regime behind, the world news claimed that it was only a matter of weeks before the communist regime collapsed there. I knew they were right; that regime was so rotten that it did not even need the Mujahideen to attack it. It was collapsing by itself. Seventy or eighty percent of the army was ready to raise a white flag and surrender to the Mujahideen. But Pakistan did not want that. A group of soldiers, who just surrendered themselves to one of these so-called Pakistani Mujahideen in Jalalabad, were all beheaded. The group who did it belonged to Mawlawi Khalis of eastern Afghanistan. Mawlawi Khalis had very close ties with the ISI.

They not only cut these soldiers along the throat but videotaped it all, which was not common at that time. Then the video was "mistakenly" leaked to the media. The communist regime of Najibulah was showed it repeatedly on Afghan TV to tell the Afghan soldiers that the Mujahideen were not against the communists, that they were "against all of you, so if you surrender, you know exactly what will happen to you." That scared the Afghan army to death and they decided to continue the fight. It worked exactly the way ISI wanted it to.

Pakistan also knew that an Afghan Mujahideen attack against the communist government was imminent, and that they were going to attack the Jalalabad base close to the border. So Pakistan planned a controlled attack, meaning they leaked the plan to the Najibulah government and let the communists know when and from which direction the attack was coming. The communist government, knowing all the details of the attack, planned an air assault to easily counter their attack. Hundreds of Mujahideen were killed, the rest were embarrassed and demoralized. This was the way Pakistan wanted to tell the west and the Islamic governments that although the Soviets had left Afghanistan the danger was still there: "so please do not stop your aid, please continue."

Although the American government lost their interest in Afghanistan quite quickly after the Soviets left Afghanistan, they were still sending some help. The Islamic countries also felt obligated not to forget their Afghan brothers. I can tell you that for the next three years Pakistan did whatever they could to keep Najibulah's government on its feet, until 1992.

Finally, like a dead body, the Najibulah government caved in under its own weight. The strongmen in the government knew that if they just left the country and let the government shutter, and let the barbaric Pakistani Mujahideen get to Kabul, there would be rivers of blood flowing through the streets of Kabul. So they surrendered the government to the Afghan-based Mujahideen, and on the top of them Ahmad Shah Masood. Now the Pakistanis saw that they were about to lose Afghanistan, along with their billion dollar blood business. Soon they sent armies of those Mujahideen, led by Gulbudin Hekmatyar. Those same Mujahideen who were not able to do anything against Najibulah's communist regime and were just basically sleeping in Pakistan, now had their orders to rush to Afghanistan and do whatever possible to defeat Masood.

That same Gulbudin, who for the last three years was just shooting a few missiles here and there every once in a while, now brought thousands of those missiles from Pakistan and randomly shot them into the city of Kabul. In one day, he shot over 1200 missiles into the city. He killed hundreds of people every day. Now, for the first time in the history of Afghan War, the Pakistani Mujahideen were taking things seriously. I remember the day on which Gulbudin shot 1200 rockets at the city of Kabul. People did not even have the time to take the bodies of their family members from the rubbles for burial. They just had to leave.

There were no cars or buses to take and leave Kabul. Tens of thousands of people were walking tirelessly without food and water toward Pakistan, the same place where Gulbudin was getting his missiles, and his orders to destroy their houses. The Kabul-Jalalabad highway was so crowded with pedestrians that the buses could not go through at all. That was likely the worst day in the history of our people. On that day as many people left Kabul as in the Soviet era, in a whole year that many people had never left our country. For Pakistan, of course, this was welcome news, because now all those people coming to Pakistan would die of hunger if the world did not help, and that meant hundreds of millions of dollars for Pakistan.

For the next three years Gulbudin Hekmatyar was busy killing the Afghans and not allowing the Afghan Mujahideen to form a powerful government. But it was not only Gulbudin who was working actively for Pakistan; the six other Pakistani Mujahideen leaders were in Kabul and, from inside the government, were trying to prevent the Afghan people from getting closer to a working government.

During this era the Pakistani government income from the Afghan war dropped substantially, and the Pakistani officials, now quite used to a luxurious lifestyle, were looking for new ways to boost their income. Gulbudeen Hekmatyar was supplied with unlimited number of missiles to attack Kabul on a daily base, while Pakistan tried to sell off Afghan natural resources from inside the government. When Kabul was burning in the flames of a war waged by the Nawaz Sharif Pakistani government, his minister Sardar Asif Ali Khan flew in representatives from foreign nations to buy into the Afghan resources for far less than it should have cost them. The heroic resistance of the Afghan people prevented Pakistan from achieving this goal, but soon the attention of the Pakistanis shifted somewhere else: the poppy fields and heroin within.

During the Soviet-Afghan war Pakistan was able to turn thousands of Afghans into spies for the ISI, and soon tens of thousands of acres of land near Pakistan was turned into poppy growing farms. This made the poppy crops easily accessible for our enemies to the south. The poppies did not require much investment or time to harvest. The only thing they needed was a force in Afghanistan to keep the Afghans like Masood busy in so-called civil war. Billions of dollars were made in a matter of months.

If the world complained about the heroin production, Pakistan would just blame the Afghans. But when it came to billions of dollars in profit, all of it went to Pakistan. That was, in the end, what triggered the creation of the Taliban. The Pakistanis knew that the Afghans were tired of war. So they created a totally unknown force, under the name of peace, a peace to let Pakistanis do there heroin production business peacefully! Pakistan had tens of thousands of Afghans in their pocket from the Afghan-Soviet war era. Many of them were orphans who had lost their families and had lived in Pakistan, alone within the refugee camps, for years, who knew no other parental touch than Pakistan's abusive hands.

Pakistan put them in front of one of their puppets Mullah Omar, and sent them in the name of peace to Afghanistan. Seemingly overnight, the Taliban marched to many different areas in Kandahar.

This really got the attention of the Afghan people. A bunch of unknown people, flying the flag of Islam but with no real history or background of military success, marching like a storm: people really thought that God must have been with them. These are the best tricks, always work in Islamic countries.

They marched to Kabul, but not to fight Massoud. Instead they attacked the base of Gulbudin Hekmatyar in Charasia, from where Gulbuden had been shooting hundreds of missiles a day. As Massoud was not able to push him back, the Taliban quickly conquered the area. Gulbudeen conveniently fled because ISI wanted that to happen.

The Taliban, now were in the center of attention inside and outside Afghanistan, and they were keep talking about peace. The best option for Massoud was to leave Kabul as a gift for peace. Then, just like when the communist coup succeeded in Afghanistan over one and half decades before, people once again were giving flowers to the Taliban soldiers in the streets. And soon, again they were awoken to the worst surprise of their lives, worse that anything they'd experienced before.

Now the ISI and Pakistani officials were really happy with the results, and safely busy with their booming heroin business. Billions were generated from the Afghan poppy, and from those billions only a small percentage was spent on the Taliban and the war to subdue the Afghan resistance. The net profit went to the corrupt ISI and Pakistani officials. Even the brutality of the Taliban and all the support they were getting from the Pakistanis was not enough to break the will of the Afghan people though; to suffocate their desire to free their country. Thus the ISI brought in Osama bin Laden, Ayman al-Zawahiri, and thousands of Arab hardliners on the run from the CIA. Thousands of more Chechen and Uzbek hardliners who were also in Pakistan to get weapons and training for their struggles against their governments were sent into Afghanistan too.

But these hardliners had their own agenda. They were so hateful towards the US and Israel that their carnivorous attitude towards freedom made them turn westward. Pakistan was not about to allow the extremists make a move against America though, as that would effectively kill the golden goose. But Bin Laden was under pressure from his followers. While the extremists were not doing anything against America and Israel physically, yet, they were training hard.

Some of their secrets were discovered by CIA agents after they interviewed some of the hardliners inside Massoud's detention centers in Panjsher. From 1998 forward things began to shift a little against Pakistan and Taliban, and with the al Qaeda attack on the USS Cole in October 2000 things got much more serious. America was alarmed and started to pressure Pakistan to make a move against Osama and his followers. But the ISI needed all of those Arabs to guard the thousands of acres of poppy fields in Afghanistan and sustain their multi-billion dollar heroin enterprise.

America offered a few hundred million dollars to the Pakistani government as operation expenses against al Qaeda leaders, but by then the heroin rich ISI did not need the money and ignored American requests. Before the attack on the USS Cole, Pakistan convinced the Americans that not only were the Taliban not bad for America, but that they were beneficial because they were creating problems for Iran and Moscow. They were sending Chechen and Uzbek rebels to create trouble for Moscow, or in another word, they were following the Red Army all the way to Moscow, something the US was quietly favoring. But after the attack on the Cole, the Americans were convinced they needed to make a move against Osama and hardliners in Afghanistan. The first thing America did, in the year 2000, was to pressure Pakistan to control the flow of weapons from Pakistan to Afghanistan. The Pakistanis got really nervous about this, knowing the restrictions would give the upper hand to Massoud and the Afghan people; that it could seriously jeopardize the ISI heroin industry.

The ISI still did not want an attack by Osama on the US to happen and wanted to prevent it at all costs. But Pakistanis knew that America did not need them anymore, like when they needed them during the Afghan-Soviet war era, and there was no way of convincing the Americans to change their mind. When they did not find another solution, finally the Arab extremists anti-American rage and the Pakistan ISI greed melted together. Pakistan gave the green light to the Arab extremists to proceed with their plan against America, with a hope that it would once again put them on the map of American friends, or the ones they needed help and support from, or at least make Americans more busy with a different problem so simply they could not control the weapon flow to Afghanistan..

When Massoud was invited by the head of the European Parliament in 2001 to address the European parliament, Massoud warned America directly that he had intelligence that a major attack against America, inside America, was imminent. This Afghan freedom fighter, whose soldiers did not even have enough to eat, with no intelligence service of his own knew things that the super-powers, with all those billion dollar budgets, did not. Though one thing that Massoud did not have intelligence about himself was that his own assassination was the precondition to Pakistan allowing the al Qaeda to attack America.

On September 9, 2001 two Arabs posing as journalists were able to arrange an interview with Massoud at his base in northern Afghanistan. They ignited explosives placed inside their video cameras. Massoud was seriously wounded and sent to Tajikistan for treatment. The ISI waited another day to make sure that Massoud would not make it, but as soon as they got word of that, al Qaeda operatives went ahead with their plans.`

It was because of these extremists that we left Afghanistan. It was because of them that millions of our innocent people were slaughtered in Afghanistan.

During the Afghan-Soviet war alone we lost two million Afghans: 100,000 thousand killed by Afghan communists, 100,000 killed by the Red army, but 1.8 million were killed by these Muslim extremists in the name of God. The majority of Afghans left Afghanistan because of these so-called Charlie's warriors, during Charlie Wilson's War and after. To see them now inside America, doing what they were doing to Afghans in Afghanistan, was extremely heartbreaking. I loved this country as much as I did my motherland, Afghanistan. This country gave me, my family, and tens of thousands of Afghans shelter at a time we were being killed left and right.

Our plane ticket was paid for; for months, even years, we were supported financially, given free medical care, free education, and free housing. More than that, in our country the only right we had was the right to die, and in this great country we were given any right an American had themselves. Our American-born kids could even run for President one day, if they wanted to. Even today, after thirty years over which Afghans got refuge in Iran, Pakistan, Saudi Arabia, and all the other Islamic countries, we could not be accepted as citizens there.

I remember that each time I watched the clips of the twin towers burning and giving in under the blaze and their own weight, it made me cry. I called everyone in the Afghan community in Seattle to get together and denounce the brutal crime committed by those extremists. I believe we were the first Afghan community, or any community, to denounce those brutal crimes against our new country and our new countrymen. I wanted to help as much as I could, and I told the entire media that.

In those days, to be honest, as an Afghan-Muslim we were also extremely concerned as to what would happen to us. Would Americans attack us here at home, because we were Muslims? In our country, an immediate slaughter would begin against any such people who dared to do the same thing to us. But instead, President Bush went on television, and warned Americans not to commit any crimes against Muslims in America. Ashcroft did the same thing, warning that any crime against Muslims would be prosecuted to the fullest extent of the law. In our eyes, America had just saved our lives once again.

I remember watching the local TV channel in the days following 9/11, when I saw an amazing interview. The news clip was showing one of the Mosques in Puget Sound, Washington, and the reporter was interviewing two American women – both white, both Christian – at the corner of the Mosque. The two were shedding tears, and said that they would stand there to ensure nobody came to attack the Muslim community in their neighborhood. They said quite clearly, that they were there to protect Muslims "Because they are our neighbors." I did not know if they knew or even they cared that the Mosque they were protecting was the worst nests of extremists in Seattle. At least a half a dozen Afghan extremists had membership there, and all were members of the most extreme Pakistani-based Islamic extremist groups Hezbi Islami Gulbudeen Hekmatyar, who hated Americans more than anything else in this world.

Just before 9/11, for example, eight missionaries were arrested in Kabul by Taliban. I believe three were Americans, and if I remember correctly, two were women from Texas. They were accused of converting Muslims to Christianity, a serious offence in all the Islamic countries, and in Afghanistan under the Taliban it meant certain death. These same friends of Gulbuden Hekmatyar sent out a newsletter to all Afghans in Puget Sound calling for their execution. And now I was watching these two American, white, female Christians, standing at the corner of that same Mosque, vowing to support these same Muslim extremists in their possible time of need. I was so stunned, and exclaimed, "What a great religion this Christianity must be. What a great people Americans are. What a great nation, what a great people!"

If you talk with Muslims in America, they always have their stories of converting Christians to Muslims. We have the freedom to talk with people and to invite them to become Muslims whenever we wish. But if you were to do the reverse in the Muslim world, you can be charged and even hanged. Even today, while we Afghans have hundreds of Mosques in America (most built with welfare money), in a community with only thirty years history, no one can build a church in Afghanistan. You do it, see what happens. As a side note, those same extremists who wrote that newsletter were hired a few years later as translators for the American army with a salary of twenty thousand dollars a month.

Sometimes I think we are too nice here, just a little bit too nice: an unbalanced kind of nice. Of course, I closely followed the news from Afghanistan and what the American government was up to after 9-11 to this date. Just days after 9/11 Colin Powell was in Pakistan where General Musharraf was busy convincing him to not attack the Taliban. Colin Powell repeated those words, with Musharraf at his side. He promised Musharraf that the Northern Alliance would not be allowed to reach Kabul. All of the sudden a new term entered the fray: *moderate Taliban*. We had millions of Afghans, in the north and the south, Pushtoons and Tajiks and Uzbeks and Hazara who hated the Taliban, who wanted to go after them, arrest them, shred them to pieces, but they were marked as the Northern Alliance, and they were prevented from doing so. We ignored all of them, and instead we began begging the Taliban for cooperation. Even when we cornered Osama bin Laden and al-Zawahiri in Tora Bora, still we did not use the angry anti-Taliban forces. Instead, we used the same forces connected to the ISI, and both Osama and al-Zawahiri were able to escape. For the first seven years after 9/11, our policy had been to beg the Taliban for peace.

When Barrack Obama came to power I hoped that American policy would change from begging the Taliban to beating the Taliban, but it became even softer. McChrystal - our new man in charge of the war in Afghanistan - came up with a surprising new policy of "winning the hearts and minds of the Afghan people". Even more surprising, it seemed that he meant more the Taliban than the majority of Afghans. Because if you want to win the hearts and minds of the millions of Afghans, then you would need to join forces with them, kick the Taliban out, and clean the country of poppies and drug lords, the only reason for this war.

His policy of winning the hearts and minds of the people of Afghanistan was interpreted as soft in my homeland; as betraying the Afghan people, and as getting even cozier with the Taliban. There was an article about McChrtystal's hearts and minds policy put out in Afghanistan during 2009. I believe they were quoting the Newsweek. In it he said that often "the shot you don't fire is more important than the one you do." Then he went on and explained that "if you encounter 10 Taliban members and kill two, you don't have eight remaining enemies. You have more like 20: the friends and relatives of the two you killed." The calculation was that for each Taliban you killed, you would create six new ones...

In an article, I wrote at the time I said that, "Now you tell me what you are going to do if you are an American soldier in Afghanistan and are faced down by ten armed Taliban killers? Are you going to allow them to kill you so you do not create 60 more Taliban for your comrades, or are you going to kill all of them?" No, really, what would you do? Of course you would allow them to shoot you if you believed in what McChrystal was saying! Thus was the policy of our new Commander-in-Chief in Afghanistan.

With these kinds of politics, we will always be in a tough slog against the Taliban, whether we win or not. You need to know the psychology of your enemies and your friends; this kind of policy does not tell the Taliban and the Afghan people what an excellent peacemaker you are. It will tell them how soft you are and how weak and vulnerable you are. It will make your enemies even more brutal, because they think you have a broken wing. Afghan extremists see fair mindedness as weakness. These policies even drive your friends away, as they fear that you will never win the battle, or the war.

So many other things have gone wrong in the past years. In 2009 we spent close to one billion dollars in Afghanistan's Presidential election. In a poor country like Afghanistan, this is just insane. The argument was that the Afghans wanted a taste of real democracy. Okay, let's agree that such an election would teach the Afghans the benefits of voting; the benefits of not solving their problems with guns. It was an excellent step forward. But later on that same year, we spent hundreds of millions more on an all but useless Afghan elder's assembly: a *Loya Jirga*...

Do you know what a *Loya Jirga* is, and what kind of power it has? In some rural areas of Afghanistan, where there is no government, in those little mountainous villages, if some dispute occurs among the villagers, some elders get together and come up with a solution to the problem. Something like, "Okay, you killed his son, so you give him two cows and one of your daughters and we'll call it even." This is what a *Loya Jirga* means.

In Afghanistan, wherever we have government, people do not rely on a *Jirga*. Secondly, the government does not allow them to solve those kinds of disputes through elderly meetings, because it challenges the authority of the government and the rule of the law. So in the history of Afghanistan, a *Loya Jirga* was never an institution to solve state or federal level problems. Only a few times in the history of Afghanistan did we have a *Jirga* that crossed state borders, but they were always phony *Jirga*'s sponsored by the government for show. In reality they did not have any power; they were just symbolic.

You can buy all the elders, and throw as many *Jirga* parties as you want, but the real power is in the hands of Taliban, all young and between 18 and 35. Any elder they want, can be killed tomorrow.

Jirgas belong to the distant past and traditionally oppose central government control and power. And this was the third such *Loya Jirga* called to order, just to make Karzai happy. Typically instead of showing up, the Taliban just shoot missiles at them. It was also funny that the American government sent officials to ensure the rights of women were being protected—without any real context, or understanding that this was only a part of the problem. Let me tell you why.

I am sure a lot of you remember that during their last year in office the Taliban blew up two statues of Buddha in Afghanistan that constituted a World Heritage site. This was the most valuable historic site in the history of our country. Even Islam itself would never recommend the demolition of such statues, which had no real religious value anymore, just historical value. But the Taliban went ahead and mercilessly did it anyways. The Taliban and al Qaeda discriminated against not only women, and history itself, but even against a statue!

We all hear about the Taliban and their abuse of women's rights. But again, the Taliban were against far more than meets the eye. During their reign, the religious police closely watched women for anything they might perceive as an indiscretion. If a woman was going out by herself to buy some food for her orphans, she would be whipped on the corner of street. If she even went out with her brother or father or husband, still she was not safe. Of course all women had their burkas on to cover themselves from head to toe, but if the wind was blowing and if she had a little hole in her socks, and a tiny bit of her skin was showing, she would be whipped in front of her brother or husband's eyes.

The man could only silently endure the pain, otherwise he would be whipped too. Now, do you think this is purely discrimination against that woman's rights? Imagine yourself walking with your wife, and a religious policeman pulled your wife away and whipped her in front of your eyes. Does this not also constitute an abuse of you as well? But that is not all there is. Those same religious police were also watching the men too. For example, if your beard was not as long as our prophet Muhammad's was, then you would be whipped too, in front of your wife or daughter, or sister, and the public. In the history of Afghanistan, at least the modern history, no one remembered any such thing .

These same police took the men away, pulled their pants down so that they could see the hair between their legs, and if it was not short enough, like our prophet Muhammad, again you would be whipped. So, when you are only looking out for the rights of one specific kind of person, you really don't understand the Taliban. This, and other reasons, is why we are on the verge of collapse in Afghanistan.

****

As you see the last pages of my book have transformed the text from a story from long ago into an illustration of what I see continuing today. I hate to do this. But I have to, because I see we are going to the wrong direction. And I see that I have to shout. You may or you may not agree with me, but look, for nine years now we have been in Afghanistan and things are moving backwards. I am an American now, I cannot see us lose there. I have already lost too much.

****

Fortunately, today, my mother is alive. She is an old lady now. That woman with the energy of a bee cannot even walk from one side of the room to the other without her cane. She still cooks though, excellently, just like always. She is so independent, that even now she does not allow anyone else to do her dishes. My Dad, the only one not in America during the 1980s and 1990s, finally arrived here two years ago. I believe he now has six kids from the new wife. And he lives just miles away from where my mother lives.

He sent messages to Mom a few times, begging her to allow him to see her just once to ask for forgiveness, because he is so old now fears he will be dead before getting the chance, but she rejected that.

I sometimes joke with her about what she would do if one day he just showed up at her door. She tells me that she would beat him on the head with her cane. I joke with her then as to why she hates Dad so much, when, at least, he never married a little six year old kid, like our Prophet Muhammad did (Ayesha was only six when our Prophet married her). "But he was a Prophet son, god wanted him to do that," she replies.

"Mother," I reply, "but my Dad was not married with more than two women at the same time, while our Prophet was married with many women at the same time, in addition to having hundreds of Kaneez." (Kaneez were women confiscated during Jihads after their families were slaughtered, used for heavy labor and also for sex).

"But he was a man of justice," she replies.

A man of Justice, yes, justice, a man of justice.

But what is justice? A march that never ends? A destiny never reached? A fight no one wins?

I think we are all in this world for justice, and we are all fighting for justice to the last day we die. Even then, we end those lives with the hope of justice awaiting us when we meet our creator.

W.W.M.D.

For years I avoided reading about Islam. Deep inside, I was not connected to my faith. I blamed much of what went on in my life, the hard times, on Islam. I knew what all Afghan children knew from when we were forced to learn about the religion over our twelve years of schooling. In the year 2002, I was in Los Angeles distributing one of my new books *Afghanistan Jihad and Sulha*, written in my native language of Dari. There I met another Afghan who provided me with a Dari translation of the Quran. I took it from him in order to be respectful, but had no plans of reading it. But during my flight back to Seattle I opened that Quran out of boredom and began to flip through it.

That was it. For the next six years I became inseparable from that book. I read it, and read it, and kept reading it. Each time I read it as if I had to pass the most important test of my life. I read it as a Muslim, as a Communist, as a Jew, as a Christian, as a Hindu, as a Buddhist, as an atheist, as a plant, as an animal, as a statue, and you name it.

It was really confusing and a very complex text, at times nearly impossible to understand, but I did not give up. I said to myself that "if this is really a book from God to us, then I must be able to overcome my misunderstandings and fi nally be able to understand it". Over time, I did. And the more I learned, the more I noticed that we Muslims are the most uninformed, the most miss informed and the most uneducated people when it comes to our religion on the face of the earth. It is not that we do not study our religion, we do, and we *Afghan hearts & minds* 200 do more so than the followers of any other religion. But, the Quran itself is not only hard to understand, but really confusing.

In addition, we Muslims are so fearful of our God, and our prophet, that we never allow ourselves to ask questions about Islam: we are reading only to believe. Fourteen hundred years of learning the Quran and Islam like that, has created a vast pane of tinted glass that is totally blocking us from understanding Islam. Now, Islam is not about the Quran, or God, or even the Prophet; it is about thousands of little fairy tales.

The Islamic world today is the most confused world on the face of the earth. We believe that Islam is a religion of peace, and we force people to believe in that, but as we all know tolerance and respect is the basic element needed for peace, and Muslims have zero tolerance and zero respect. An unknown pastor in Florida claims that he will burn a copy of the Quran(Sep. 2010), and we take to the streets all over the world in violent protests. We start burning the fl ags of any European and American country, because they are Christian countries, and if a Christian pastor is burning our Quran then we believe it justifi es going after any Christian. The world is lucky that we Muslims do not have the military might of America or China or Europe, or Russia, otherwise we might very well kill millions of Christians over the issue... but yet our religion is a religion of peace, and you better believe it!

Now, how many people can devote six years of their lives to read and understand the Quran, especially when even six years would not be enough for the vast majority of Muslims - many do not have the basic skills to even read Quran through once, and even when they do, they are too afraid to question as they read. That is the core of our Islamic problems. And since we are 1.2 billion people strong in the world, our problem can become the problems of the entire rest of the world. Today the world is so connected that I can say *we are all each other's neighbors*, and in a world that is so small and so connected we can no longer tolerate the heat of extreme ideologies.

That is why after six years of readying the Quran; I spent another two years of studying the first five hundred years of Islam, and as a human being felt obligated to write a book about my religious journey into the texts. I did.

As I was finishing my manuscript (W.W.M.D – What would Mohamad do), I was watching that the situation in Afghanistan deteriorating and the Taliban, the drug warlords of the ISI, and the extremists gain the upper-hand. I suddenly postponed the completion of my W.W.M.D. and started writing *Afghan hearts & minds.* "I can publish my W.W.M.D. twenty years from now and it would still not be too late, but for the book you are reading right now, even a month from now it could be late." I thought.